Tapas

from the Spanish kitchen

Tapas
from the Spanish kitchen

EDITED BY **Lidelsur**

PRODUCED BY **LaMetro.fox** / *Equipo 28*

COORDINATION, EDITING & PRODUCTION
Isabel Lovillo y Anselmo Valdés

TEXTS
Anselmo Valdés, Diego Solís Farce, José Manuel y Tito Tenorio

TRANSLATION
Donald Scrimgeour

PHOTOGRAPHS
Manolo Manosalbas, A.Valdés, Adriana Gutiérrez, Luis G. Cervantes,
Margarita Asuar, Turismo Andaluz, Private archives

DESIGN & LAYOUT
Cristina Peralta / **LaMetro.fox**

PRINTED BY
Egondi Artes Gráficas

ISBN: 978-84-939069-1-7
DEPÓSITO LEGAL: SE-4738-2011

The object of this book is to show dishes from the Spanish Kitchen presented in their smallest gastronomic form: la Tapa. The general ingredients and the basic preparation are described, leaving the reader free rein to his imagination, in relation to the products available in his local market and to his knowledge and, above all, to the extent of his desire to please the palate of his fellow diners.

Our thanks go to Diego Solís Farce, for his good work and excellent teaching; to Dani García, a maestro; to the De Rojas family of the Grupo La Raza; to Alberto Varela; to Tito and José Manuel Tenorio, from the Tasca Tenorio in Tenerife; to the Santarúa restaurant in Candás; La Galana in Gijón; to Casa Latino in León; to San Cristóbal in Córdoba; to La Ponderosa in Cuenca; La Marisina in Madrid; to Casa Manolo in Punta Umbría; to Es Pla in Fornells; to the Kursaal in Donostia; to the Casa Rosita in Cambados; to Baserri in Pamplona; to Sancho Panza, Albarama, Forties and Casa Moreno in Sevilla; to Castañeda and Chiquito in Granada… and to so very many professionals and places for teaching us and enabling some of us to become veritable "mini-chefs".

Anselmo Valdés

INDEX

Presentation

According to the Royal Spanish Academy, tapa is a small portion of food, served as an accompaniment to a drink. This definition is interpreted differently according to how it is presented in different parts of Spain and may be termed poteo, alifara, pincho, or tapa.

This way of eating has been going on for centuries, based initially in a small accompaniment such as olives, cheeses and cured pork products. In fact something to accompany a glass of wine, which could cover the glass in which it was served.

In the course of time and through the changes brought by tradition and good food in Spanish kitchens, small portions of prepared foods began to appear, with a view to their being savoured as aperitifs but never becoming confused with typical fast food.

This tradition of presenting a small piece of food to accompany a drink so that the alcohol didn't go straight to one's head dates back to King Alfonso X the Wise. There is also an anecdote concerning King Alfonso XIII, when he visited the famous Ventorrillo de El Chato in Cadiz, which describes using a slice of jam to cover the glass of wine he was offered, in order to avoid any sand getting into the liquid. Cervantes also refers to this habit in his "Don Quixote" as llamativos and Quevedo uses avisillo.

Each region of Spain has its own type of cuisine and tapas, according to its best local products, such as fish, vegetables, meats, rice ... but there are two dishes which have won their place around the globe in the gastronomic world: paella and gazpacho. Richard Ford, in his book "Gathering from Spain" (1846), wrote the following about gazpacho:

> A type of vegetable soup, which constitutes
> the staple diet of the inhabitants of the
> hottest areas of Spain in Summer.

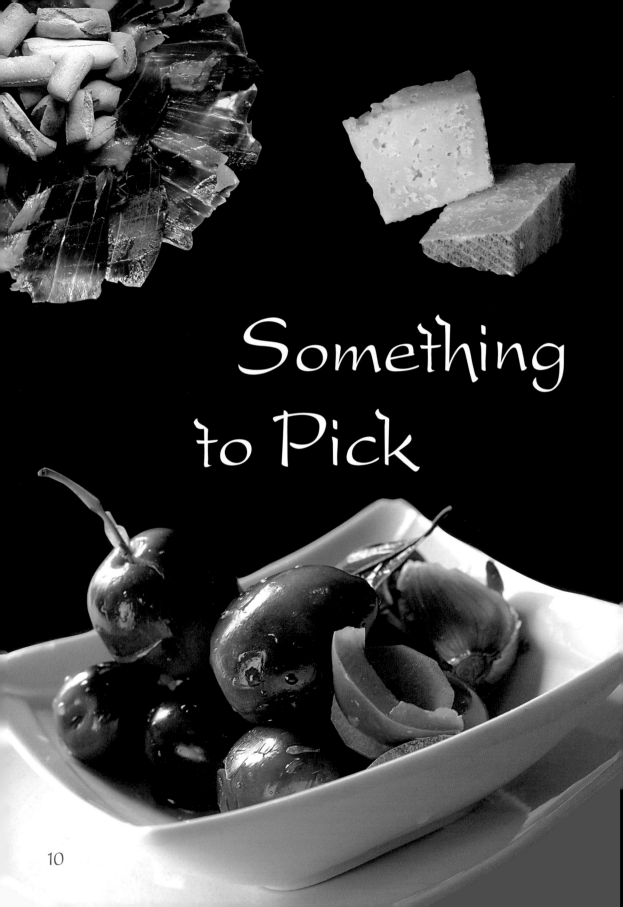

Something to Pick

This first section talks about foods that help to whet one's appetite, eat lightly, or make waiting a bit more agreeable. These products can vary a lot, ranging from cured pork cuts to pickles and olives on a cocktail stick, canapés and dressed morsels. Maintaining coherence between the tastes to be mixed is very important, as well as the presentation and the way in which they will be eaten. Ideally it should be tasted in a single mouthful, not have a sauce and not need a fork, to make it informal, nimble and quick. Thus cured ham, cheese, charcuterie in general, steamed or boiled shellfish and olives and their variants are the kings of the aperitifs. Cured ham requires a good support for the leg, a very sharp knife, calm and style in the cutting and, of course, a good ham. The slices of ham should be placed on a plate alongside each other but not piled up and in a single layer, just as with *caña de lomo, salchichón ...* which also have another interesting form of presentation, being diced. In the case of cheese, each bit should include a little rind, as in most cases, the characteristics that define its flavour, such as maturity, mould and other information, are concentrated therein. The best accompaniments for these aperitifs are different types of handmade breads or picos (small crisp breads). The accompanying drinks, whether wine in the form of reds, whites, clarets, manzanillas, finos ... pilsner or lager beers, or other drinks, should be treated with equal respect and care with regard to their temperature and flavour and, above all, be served in an appropriate glass.

Dressed

Peppers with Melva
(Frigate Mackerel)

Ingredients

Red peppers.
Canned melva, tuna or similar.
A large tomato.
A spring onion.
Virgin olive oil.
Balsamic vinegar.
Salt.

Roast the red peppers in the oven, or grill them. Cover them and leave them to cool, so that they "sweat". Once cool, peel and cut into strips. Chop the spring onion finely and dress with balsamic vinegar, oil and salt. Mix everything well. Serve on a bed of tomato slices, which have been seasoned, and sprinkle some pieces of melva canned in virgin olive oil on top.

Dressed

Prawns

Cook the prawns in salted water with a bay leaf. Peel them and cut them into medium sized bits. Dice the tomato, the pepper and the onion and add them to the prawns. Make a dressing with the oil, vinegar and salt and pour over the salad. Serve cold.

Ingredients

Prawns.
A Tomato.
A green pepper.
An onion.
A bay leaf.
Virgin olive oil.
Vinegar.
Salt.

on Toast with Ventresca

Ingredients

Ventresca (belly of tuna).
Roast peppers.
A large slice of toasted bread.
Virgin olive oil.
Vinegar.
Salt.

Papas «Aliñá»
(PotatoSalad)

Ingredients

New Potatoes.
A medium sized white onion.
Virgin olive oil.
Vinegar.
Parsley.
Salt.

Put the washed potatoes in their skins in a pot. Cover with plenty of water and place over the heat. When they begin to boil, lower the heat so that they cook slowly and don't break up. Leave them to boil for 5 minutes, add a handful of salt and finish cooking over a low heat. Place the potatoes on a draining board and while still hot, peel them and put them in the refrigerator for 1 hour. When cold, cut the potatoes into slices and put them in a large serving dish. Chop the onion and the parsley. Place in a bowl and add the olive oil, vinegar and a pinch of salt. Mix well and pour over the potatoes. As a complement, one might add crumbled tuna, some hard-boiled egg, or olives; but always finely chopped and mixed with the vinaigrette.

Stuffed

Ingredients

Large stoned olives.
Anchovies.
Strips of piquillo peppers
(small hot red pepper).
Grated orange rind.
Virgin olive oil.
Vinegar.
Garlic.
Sal.

Introduce a piece of anchovy and a strip of pepper into each olive, letting them stick out at each end. Prepare a vinaigrette with approximately three parts olive oil and one of vinegar. Add a clove of crushed garlic and the grated orange rind. Let the olives marinate in the vinaigrette for 1 hour or more. Serve with a little salt to taste and a little grated orange rind.

Wrapped in Pickled Anchovy Fillets

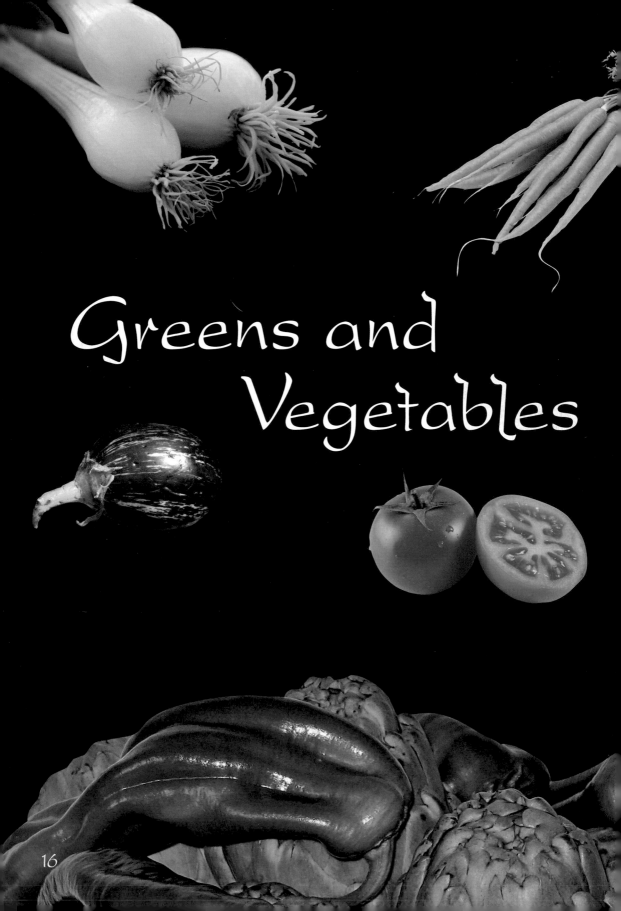

Greens and Vegetables

There is a saying in
Spanish that runs
*"With fruit and
vegetables, life
lasts longer".* Using vegetables and greens,
both in summer and winter, results in our eating habits being
healthy and in reducing obesity and its associated diseases.
Their principal contribution is in vitamins, minerals, fibres and cellulose
and is always related to their colours - Vitamin A in the yellow and red and
C in the green ... - their low fats, their hydrates and other vitamin content
make them a vital food and protector of our health. Greens and vegetables
should be washed carefully and even scrubbed, according to whether they
are leaves, roots or tubers. The latter should not be peeled or scraped, as
the skin contains a large quantity of vitamins and other nutritious elements.
In order for greens and vegetables to retain their properties and their flavour,
they should be put straight into boiling water, or even better, be steamed or
roasted in their skins. Salt should only be added at the end of the cooking
process, as it tends to harden the water. There are green-leafed vegetables
(low in calories and high in food value): lettuce, chicory and chard...; yellow
vegetables (rich in carotene): carrot, pumpkin...; vegetables of other colours
(rich in vitamin C and in B complex): beetroot, onion, tomato...; tubers
and roots: potato...Vegetables are very necessary for our health
and, even though the highest vitamin and mineral content
is in the raw vegetable, we should try it first, for not all
stomachs can tolerate it in this form. Thus boiled,
steamed or cooked with other foods, may be
the best form of consumption.

ofOrangeandBacalao

Ingredients

An orange.
A tender spring onion.
Salt cod.
Black olives.
Virgin olive oil.
Walnuts.
Mint.
Balsamic vinegar.

Wash and peel the orange and remove the skin from the segments. Chop the spring onion and crumble the salt cod, having previously cut it into very fine slices on a board. Prepare a vinaigrette with the Balsamic vinegar, virgin olive oil, the walnuts and mint. To present the salad, place the ingredients in a shallow dish and top it off with the crumbled slices of bacalao and a drizzle of vinaigrette. It is advisable to soak all the ingredients of this original salad some time before serving.

ofVentresca withAvocado

Ingredients

A variety of lettuces.
An Avocado.
A Tomato.
Belly of tuna in olive oil.
Chopped almonds.
Salt in flakes.
Balsamic vinegar.
Virgin olive oil.

Wash and cut up the lettuces. Cut half the tomato in cubes (reserving the other half). Also cube the avocado. Lightly toast the almonds in a frying pan with a few drops of olive oil. Place the ingredients in a cylinder in layers, first the lettuces, then the tomato and avocado. On top, place the tuna fillets, the toasted almonds and the flaked salt. Now dress the salad, starting with the olive oil and continuing with the cream of Balsamic vinegar, which will not only act as a dressing but also give a decorative touch, given its characteristically dense texture. Serve with the half of tomato reserved previously, cut into segments.

Salads

ofPastawithCherries

Ingredients

A variety of lettuces.
Fettuccini.
Anchovies.
Cherries.
A carrot.
Cherry tomatoes.
Virgin olive oil.
Vinegar.
Salt.

Cook the fettuccini in plenty of water, with salt and a little oil and remove once *al dente.* On a plate, place the lettuces, the cherry tomatoes cut in half, the grated carrot, the cherries cut in slices and the fettuccini. Prepare a vinaigrette with the oil, vinegar, salt and finely chopped anchovies and dress the salad generously.

ofPasta
withOlives

Ingredients

A pasta of your choice.
Cherry tomatoes.
Black olives.
Grated cheese.
An onion.
Raisins.
Pine nuts.
Parsley.
Virgin olive oil.
Balsamic Vinegar.
Oregano.
Salt.

Boil the pasta in a litre and a half of water, with salt and a little oil. Once the water begins to boil, cook till it is *al dente* (about 5/8 minutes). Finely chop the onion and parsley and add two measures of oil to one of vinegar, the raisins, the pine nuts, oregano and a pinch of salt. Mix well and abundantly dress the salad, made up of the pasta, the tomatoes diced in four and the seedless black olives cut in half. Sprinkle with grated cheese.

Broad
Beans

with CuredHam

Ingredients

Broad beans.
A spring onion.
Jamón serrano
(cured ham) with its fat.
Virgin olive oil.
Parsley.

Chop the spring onion and place it in the pre-heated olive oil, together with the broad beans, over a low heat. Cover well and cook slowly, stirring from time to time, so that the ingredients don't stick. Once the beans are tender, add the ham cut in fine slices and also in cubes. Stir everything and cover until just cooked. Sprinkle with parsley and serve.

Ingredients

Wild asparagus.
An egg.
Bread.
Garlic.
Paprika.
Virgin olive oil.
Vinegar.
Salt.

Casserole
of Green Asparagus

Cut off the tips of the asparagus and cook them in salt and water. In a frying pan with hot oil, fry the whole garlic cloves and a slice of bread. Crush the garlic and the bread in a mortar. Add a spoonful of paprika and some vinegar and mix well. Pour this mixture into an earthenware dish and arrange the asparagus tips on top. Crack an egg (optional) into the dish, season to taste and place in the oven for 5 minutes. Serve hot.

23

Ingredients

1 kilo of ripe tomatoes.
Half a cucumber.
1 green pepper.
1 small clove of garlic.
200 ml. of water.
Virgin olive oil.
Vinegar.
Salt.

Peel the tomatoes and the
cucumber and chop them up,
together with the green pepper.
Place everything in a blender,
including the garlic, the oil,
the vinegar, the salt and
the water and blend.
There should be half
as much vinegar as oil.
Serve very cold.

Gazpacho

Salmorejo

Ingredients

Crumbled stale bread.
1½ kilos of ripe tomatoes.
2 cloves of garlic.
Virgin olive oil.
Vinegar.
Sal.

Soak the crumbled stale bread and drain. Mix this with the skinned tomatoes and the garlic and crush it in a mortar to attain a compact and uniform mixture (or use a blender) Mix with the oil, the vinegar and salt until it forms a thick sauce. To serve, add small cubes of cured ham, chopped hard-boiled egg and virgin olive oil. Place a mint leaf on top as decoration.

Ingredients

Peas.
New potatoes.
A sachet of saffron.
An onion.
Thick slices of bacon.
White wine.
Virgin olive oil.
Salt.
Optional: some strands of saffron.

Cook the peas in plenty of water in a saucepan with a little white wine. Add a slice of chopped bacon and cook for 15-20 minutes. When the peas are halfway through the cooking process, add the potatoes, cut into pieces, and salt to taste. At the same time, fry the finely chopped onion and the remainder of the bacon in a little olive oil in a frying pan. Once golden, add some sprigs of saffron (optional) to enhance the flavour. Remove from the heat and pour over the contents of the saucepan. Add the sachet of saffron and continue to cook until the peas and potatoes are done.

Peas
withBaconandPotatoes

Spinach
withChickpeas

Ingredients

Spinach.
Chickpeas.
Garlic.
Slices of bread.
Paprika.
Cumin seeds.
Virgin olive oil.
Vinegar.
1 chilli.
Salt.

Put the chickpeas to soak overnight, or buy them already cooked. If the spinach is fresh, then it should be washed well, to get rid of all the earth. (Frozen spinach can be used). Cover the spinach with water and cook for about 10 minutes over a low heat. To one side, in a frying pan, add some oil and fry the whole garlic cloves in their skins, together with the pieces of bread. Remove the bread once it has turned golden and the pan from the heat, once the garlic is golden. Place the fried bread, vinegar, fried garlic, cumin and chilli to taste in a mortar and crush. Once the oil in the pan has cooled a little, add the paprika and the mixture from the mortar and fry lightly, finally adding the cooked and chopped spinach and the cooked chickpeas. Fry gently together for about 10 minutes. Season and serve on slices of fried bread, sprinkled with a little dry paprika.

Ratatouille

withEgg

Ingredients

Wash and dice the courgette and the aubergine. Clean the peppers well, removing all the seeds and cut into strips. Chop the onion and slice the garlic. Scald the tomatoes, remove the skins and dice them. In a saucepan with a little oil, fry the garlic and onions over a moderate heat for a couple of minutes. Add the peppers and continue to cook for a further 5 minutes or so. Incorporate the courgette and the aubergine for a couple of minutes without letting the onion burn and then add the tomatoes. Let everything cook for about another 15 minutes, until the tomato is cooked and the liquid reduces. Add the salt, bring the mixture to the boil quickly and remove from the heat. Serve with a fried egg.

Tomatoes.

Onion.

Courgette.

Aubergine.

Green pepper.

Garlic.

Virgin olive oil.

Salt.

An egg.

Artichokes
withCuredHam

Ingredients

Artichokes.
Jamón serrano (cured ham).
Onion.
Lemon.
Virgin olive oil.
Salt.

Remove the stalks and the hardest leaves of the artichokes. Bring a pan with plenty of salted water and the juice of a lemon (to prevent the artichokes going black) to the boil. When the water starts to boil put in the cut artichokes and cook until tender. This takes about 30 minutes. Remove them and place aside. Turn the chopped onion in a frying pan, where the oil is not too hot and when it begins to turn golden, add the cured ham, cut in strips. Sauté it and then add the artichokes. Add a little water and let it boil for a couple of minutes.
Serve immediately.

Minipizza

of Seta (Wild Mushroom)

Ingredients

One large wild mushroom.
Tomato.
Cheese for melting.
Oregano.
Chorizo. (Spanish spicy sausage)
Cured ham.
White pepper.
Virgin olive oil.
Salt.

Rinse the mushroom well in cold water. Peel and dice the tomato. Dice the ham, the chorizo and the cheese. Flatten the mushroom gently on a smooth surface. Put a layer of diced tomato on it and then add the chorizo and the ham. Sprinkle with a little pepper, cover with the cheese and place in the oven for about 10 minutes at around 180°C. Then grill until the cheese turns golden. Before serving, trickle a little virgin olive oil over the top and sprinkle with the oregano.

Grilled Mushrooms

Ingredients

Mushrooms.
Garlic.
Parsley.
Chives.
Lemon.
Virgin olive oil.
Salt.
A bouquet of lettuces.

Pour a substantial dash of olive oil into a pan and add the chopped garlic, salt, finely chopped parsley and a few drops of lemon juice. Bring to the boil. Meanwhile, remove the stalks from the mushrooms and place the mushrooms face down on the *plancha* (iron grill) over a high heat. When they are done, turn them over and cook for a further 5 minutes. Then pour over the dressing made previously. Decorate with chopped fresh chives and accompany the dish with a bouquet of different lettuces.

Asparagus
with a Spinach Sauce

Ingredients

Extra thick white asparagus.
Spinach.
Yellow cheese.
Smoked white cheese.
Cooking cream.
Diced almonds.
Garlic.
Virgin olive oil.
Salt.

Chop the garlic and fry it in oil in a frying pan until it turns golden. Add the white cheese and the almonds until they are toasted and the cheese has melted. Add the spinach (previously cooked) and sauté all the ingredients, seasoning to taste. Incorporate the cream and let it boil for 2 minutes. To serve: place the asparagus on a plate; cover it with the yellow cheese and the sauce prepared above. Cook au gratin in the microwave for 3 minutes and serve.

Escalivada

Ingredients

Peppers.
Aubergines.
Tomatoes.
Onion.
Vinegar.
Virgin olive oil.
Course sea salt.

Wash and dry the peppers, the aubergines and the tomatoes. Preheat the oven to around 200°C. Place the aubergines (make some incisions in the skin), the peppers and the onion on a baking tray, sprinkle with virgin olive oil and put it in the oven. Cook for 25 minutes at a temperature of around 180°C. Then add the tomatoes, turn the other vegetables and leave everything for a further half hour. When they are all done, let everything cool so as to be able to remove the skin and seeds from the peppers and the aubergines. Also remove the outer layers of the onion. Once all the vegetables have been skinned and the seeds removed, cut everything in strips and place in a serving dish with a pinch of course sea salt, the oil from the roasting and a few drops of vinegar. Serve on slices of toasted bread.

Aubergines
auGratin

Ingredients

A large aubergine.
Minced meat.
Grated cheese.
A red pepper.
An onion.
Milk.
Flour.
Pepper.
Garlic.
Parsley.
Virgin olive oil.
Salt.

Cut the aubergine in half and put it in a pan with water. Place it over the heat for about 10 minutes and then prick it to see if it is soft. Remove from the heat, scoop out the pulp and set aside. Meanwhile fry the onion, red pepper, garlic and parsley over a low heat. Add the minced meat and cook for about 3 minutes. Then add the pulp of the aubergine, the milk, the flour and season to taste. Let it cook for a few more minutes till it thickens. Remove from the heat; stuff the mixture into the aubergine shell and cover with grated cheese. Return to the oven for a few minutes to cook au gratin. Serve hot.

Ingredients

Piquillo peppers
(Small hot red peppers).
Vinegar.
Garlic.
Sugar.
Virgin olive oil.
Salt.

Place the garlic, cut into thin slices, in a frying pan with a lot of oil. When it begins to turn golden, add the piquillo peppers, salt, sugar or molasses and plenty of vinegar. Let everything cook, at first on a medium heat, then turning down to low. This dish is perfect eaten on its own, or as an accompaniment to fried eggs with chips, greens, or *migas...* and, above all, with grilled meats.

Pimientos
del Piquillo

35

Stuffed Peppers

Ingredients

Large peppers.
Minced meat.
Grated cheese.
Tomato sauce.
Sweet corn.
White wine.
Onion.
Garlic.
Virgin olive oil.
Black pepper.
Salt.

Poach the onion and the garlic in a frying pan with a little oil. When the onion is transparent, add the minced meat, the white wine, salt and pepper and cook over a low heat. When the meat starts to cook, incorporate the tomato sauce and cook over a low heat for 5 minutes. Then remove from the heat and add a beaten egg and the sweet corn, mixing everything very well. Meanwhile, cut off the top part of the peppers and remove the seeds. Cover them with a little oil and put them in the oven until they are almost done. Remove them and fill them with the cooked meat mixture. To finish, sprinkle them with grated cheese and give them a quick blast in the oven.

Stuffed Onion

Ingredients

A large onion.
Cooked meat.
Rice.
A hard-boiled egg.
Tomato sauce.
White wine.
Parsley.
Flour. Garlic.
Virgin olive oil. Salt.

Remove the outer layers of the onion and with the help of a scoop, clean out the pulp and fill the hole with a mixture made up of the meat, the hard-boiled egg, very finely chopped onion, cooked rice and a little tomato sauce. Fry the onion in plenty of oil until it is browned on all sides. In a frying pan, prepare a sauce with the remainder of the onion pulp, garlic, parsley, half a glass of white wine and tomato sauce. Pour all this over the stuffed onion, season to taste and cook it over a low heat until it is ready.

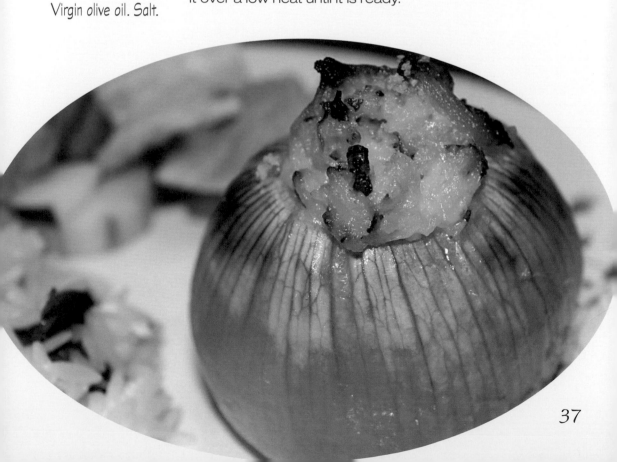

Eggs

This is a f...d rich in proteins and of high organic value. The saying goes that nobody will satiate his or her appetite with a single egg. More recently, it seems consumption has dropped, as eggs contribute to an increase in cholesterol but if levels are normal, one can eat up to one a day and if not normal, then one can dispense with the yoke. The most commonly consumed is the chicken's egg but to-day eggs of other species are also commercialised, such as quail, duck and even ostrich eggs. It is an excellent food when its value for money is taken into account. The egg is a basic ingredient for cooking, not only because of its versatility but also because of the characteristic taste it contributes to other foodstuffs and its other properties: it is frothy, an emulsifier, a colouring, binding, a thickener, a clotting agent, adhesive, a clarifier and gives a shiny finish to surfaces. Handling an egg is important. From the moment of purchase we should observe certain procedures: make sure the shell is clean and is not cracked or broken, avoid brusque changes in temperature, don't wash before storing, although it is advisable to wash them with water before use, always store in the refrigerator, discard any that smell or have an odd taste, mould on the shell or an abnormal appearance. If the inside of the egg has a small bloodstain, or the white is cloudy, this is no problem. Avoid cracking the egg on an edge and one shouldn't separate the yoke from the white using the shell. If we want to test the freshness of an egg, as a norm, the egg will sink to the bottom of a container with water and as the days go by, it will begin to rise to the surface.

ScrambledEggs
withTruffles

Ingredients

Truffles.
Eggs.
Garlic.
A slice of toasted bread.
Virgin olive oil.
Salt.

Cut the truffles in fine slices. Put a little oil in a frying pan, add the chopped garlic and cook over a low heat, till it turns golden. Add the truffles and let them cook. Season to taste and add the eggs and stir until they thicken. Serve on slices of toasted bread.

EggStuffed

withTuna

Ingredients

An egg.
Tuna.
Mayonnaise.
Chives.
Vinegar.
Salt.

Boil the egg in water with a little vinegar. Once hard, remove from the water, leave to cool and peel carefully. Cut the egg in half and remove the yoke. Place the yoke, the strained tuna and quite a lot of mayonnaise in a bowl. Mix everything well with a fork and fill the egg white halves. To serve, place the eggs with the stuffing side up on a plate and sprinkle with the chopped chives. Consume accompanied by an ice-cold beer.

Ingredients

Hard-boiled eggs.
Smoked salmon.
Salmon roe.
Cocktail sauce.
Onion.
Capers.

Cut the eggs in half and remove the yokes. In a bowl, mix the yokes, onion, finely chopped capers and the cocktail sauce. Fill the whites with the mixture and add some thin strips of salmon. To serve, decorate with the salmon roe. As an option, one can substitute the salmon for other types of roe or smoked fish, or even add these.

EggsStuffed
withSalmon

FriedEgg
with JamónSerrano

Ingredients

An egg.
Cured ham.
Potatoes
Virgin olive oil.

Peel and cut the potatoes and fry in very hot oil until they begin to turn golden. Before serving, return them to the hot oil and let them turn quite golden. Break the egg into a bowl and later fry it in the oil. When serving, place the egg on a base of fried potatoes and cover generously with slices of cured ham.

Spanish
Omelette

Ingredients

Potatoes.
Eggs.
Milk.
Virgin olive oil.
Salt.

Wash and either cut the potatoes in slices, or cubes. Once the oil is hot, add the previously salted potatoes and fry in a two-sided Spanish omelette pan. Once the potatoes are golden, remove from the heat and strain in a colander or place them on a plate with kitchen paper. Beat the eggs with a little salt and add the potatoes. Mix well with a little milk. On a low heat, pour two teaspoons of olive oil into the frying pan to cover the bottom and reheat. Add the potato and egg mixture. Keep stirring and shake the pan so that the *tortilla* doesn't stick. When it thickens place the other half of the pan over it and flip. Remove once it is golden on both sides. Serve hot. As an alternative, one can also add other ingredients that will give additional flavours like, cured ham, garlic, onion, mint…

BrokenEggs
withFoieGras

Ingredients

A Potato.
Duck foie gras.
An egg.
A Russet apple.
A sweet onion.
Salt.

Cut and fry the potato. Meanwhile separately, mix together the chopped foie, the chopped apple and the sweet onion, scramble together with an egg and season to taste. To serve, arrange the fried potatoes on a plate in the form of a nest and carefully place the other ingredients on top of them.

BrokenEggs
withDelaVeraPaprika

Ingredients

Eggs.
A Potato.
Onion.
De la Vera paprika.
Virgin olive oil.
Salt.

Cut the potato into slices and fry until crisp and juicy so that when they are carved with the egg, they mix well. Meanwhile, julienne the onion and sauté it in the same oil. Now, place the eggs in cold oil and leave until almost cooked but ensure the yoke remains soft. Mix the potatoes, salt and onion together, place the eggs on top and carve. Serve with a sprinkling of sweet paprika and hot De la Vera paprika.

Eggs

alaFlamenca

Ingredients

An egg.
Peas.
Potatoes.
Morrón peppers.
Chorizo.
Cured ham.
Crushed tomatoes.
An onion.
Garlic.
Virgin olive oil.
Salt.

This dish can range from the simplicity of the photo (broad beans, cured ham and egg), to more complicated variations, although normally it would contain the ingredients indicated. Peel and dice the potatoes and fry them in hot oil. Set aside. Chop the garlic and onion and fry in the same pan but in less oil. Then add the crushed tomato and after 5 minutes, add the peas and stir for a further 5 minutes over a low heat. Add the chopped morron peppers and the fried potatoes and continue to cook over a low heat for 10 minutes, stirring from time to time and then season to taste. When everything is ready, transfer the mixture to an earthenware casserole, crack an egg on top and arrange the slices of chorizo around the yoke and on top of the slices of cured ham. Place in the oven for about 5 minutes, at a high temperature, till the white of egg thickens. Remove from the oven and serve immediately.

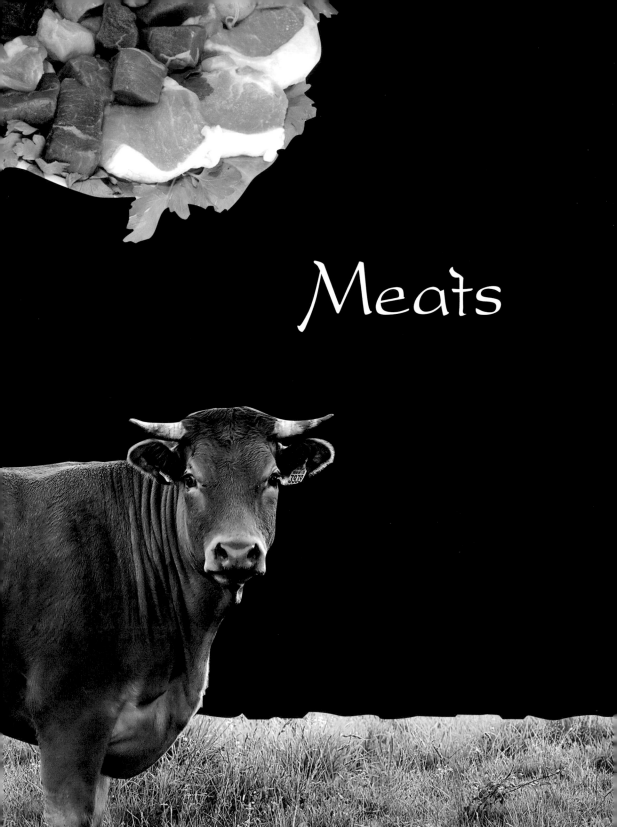

Meats

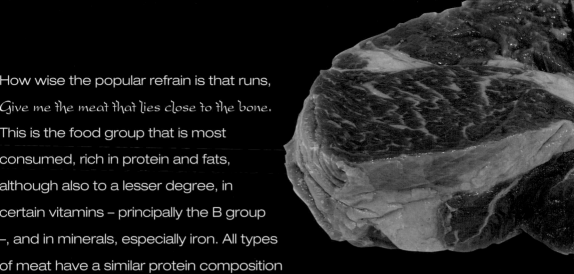

How wise the popular refrain is that runs, *Give me the meat that lies close to the bone.* This is the food group that is most consumed, rich in protein and fats, although also to a lesser degree, in certain vitamins – principally the B group –, and in minerals, especially iron. All types of meat have a similar protein composition and what really differentiates them is the quality of their fat.

Those with more saturated fats are less good for your health. Meat doesn't contain fibre and greasy unsaturated fats predominate In its fat. Nutritionists estimate that we should eat a maximum of one small fillet a day, the most consumed being: pork, beef, poultry, lamb and goat... It is important to highlight some tips/tricks on the handling and treatment of this group. One should never wash meat. If you have to remove something, do it with a damp cloth. Season once fried or roasted. If storing in the fridge, don't cover with aluminium foil or transparent film; only with waxed paper (such as used by butchers). If you think it might be a bit tough in a stew, put a cork in the pot, as it cooks. Take off as much fat as you can and remove from the fridge some 4/5 hours before preparing. Steaks turn out better if brushed with a little oil a few hours before. Finally, if you want to use minced meat and don't have any breadcrumbs, you can use grated potato as a substitute. You will see and savour the results. Cooking with meat was already described in the Middle Ages in the *Libre de Sent Soví*, in the XVIth century *Libro del Coch* by Mestre Robert and in the XVIIth century *El Arte de la Cocina,* by Martínez Montiño, where different ways of roasting, braising and frying are highlighted. In all of them, the principal dish at a banquet was always a large roast.

Ingredients

Oxtail.
An Onion.
A Ripe tomato.
A Carrot.
Red wine.
Beef stock.
Garlic.
Pepper.
Parsley.
Bay Leaf.
Potatoes.
Virgin olive oil.
Salt.

Clean all the fat off the tail, cut into bits, season with salt and pepper, roll in flour and brown in oil in a casserole. Remove from the heat and set aside. Cut and poach the onion, tomato and garlic in the same oil. Add the bay leaf, together with the sliced carrot. Leave for a few minutes to let the vegetable soften. Season to taste, incorporate the oxtail pieces and cover with the red wine and the stock. When it starts to boil, skim off the foam, cover and simmer for 1 hour over a low heat. Once tender, remove from the heat, put the sauce through a food mill (or blend) and place the ingredients in a serving dish. Serve the oxtail accompanied by fried potatoes cut in slices and parsley.

Rabo de Toro
(Oxtail)

Ingredients

Fresh sausages.
An onion.
Garllc.
White wine.
Black pepper.
A Bay leaf.
Virgin olive oil.

In a little oil, poach the garlic and finely chopped onion over a low heat. Add the sausages, the bay leaf and the pepper. Sauté for a while and then cover with white wine. Cook over a medium heat for about 15-20 minutes, until the wine begins to evaporate. When ready to serve, accompany with fried potatoes or white rice.

Sausages
in White Wine

Beef
Hamburger

Mix the meat with the garlic, parsley and salt. Once cooked, prepare the mini hamburger with the cheese, the caramelized onion and the quail's egg. Serve to taste with sweet mustard and ketchup, to which a touch of curry powder has been previously added and potato chips. To caramelise the onion, cut it in strips and sweat over medium heat, adding sugar or palm honey to taste.

Ingredients

A small hamburger roll.

Minced beef.

A quail's egg.

Caramelized onion.

A stick of yellow cheese.

Garlic. Parsley. Salt.

Sugar.

Palm honey (optional).

Sweet mustard.

Ketchup with curry flavouring.

Potato crisps.

Ingredients

Skirt of lamb.
Baking potatoes.
Fino wine from Jerez.
Onions.
Garlic.
Pâté of Iberian pork.
Virgin olive oil.
Ginger. Pepper.
A bay leaf.
Salt.
Red pepper.

Stuffed
Lamb

Clean the fat off the skirt and spread it out on a board. Season to taste. Generously spread it with pâté and roll it up. Tie the roll with esparto cord (or string) and brown it all over in virgin olive oil. Set aside. Stew the finely chopped onion, the crushed garlic cloves and the bay leaf in oil in a casserole and sprinkle with ginger. Then pour over the Fino wine and let the sauce reduce a little. Submerge the lamb in the sauce and cook for approximately 25 minutes until no more juice comes out, when you prick it with a skewer. Remove the lamb. Blend the sauce and pass it through a food mill. Once the lamb is cold, take off the esparto cord and carve in 2 cm thick slices. Serve hot, covered with sauce and accompanied by baked potatoes that have been prepared in the oven with onion, red pepper, salt, and extra virgin olive oil. Decorate with mint and parsley.

Cheek

of Iberian Pork

Remove all the fibrous bits and the fat. Place the olive oil, thyme and cloves in a pressure cooker and place over a high heat. Once the fat is hot, add the chopped onion, garlic, carrot, green pepper and tomato and poach. Next, add the chopped meat and turn until brown all over. Add red wine and water to cover, season to taste and cover the pressure cooker. Timing will depend on the make of pressure cooker but always leave it on low. Once stewed, remove the pieces of meat carefully and blend all the vegetables, to acquire a fine sauce. Serve on a bed of mashed potato and decorate with fried onions or greens.

Ingredients

Cheek of Iberian pork.
Onion.
Carrot.
Tomato.
Green pepper.
Garlic.
Thyme.
Cloves.
Red wine.
Virgin olive oil.
Salt.
Pepper.

Meatballs

In a bowl, mix the minced meat, a clove of chopped garlic, parsley, a drizzle of white wine and set aside for 15 minutes. Add the crumbled bread, a beaten egg, salt and pepper and mix well. Form little balls with this mixture and roll them in flour. Fry in abundant and very hot oil till they brown and then place them in a casserole. In a frying pan, fry the onion and chopped garlic and once golden, add the chopped tomatoes, leaving them to cook for 5 minutes before adding glass of white wine. Boil for 3 minutes and then put this sauce through a food mill. Serve the sauce and the meatballs separately, or pour the sauce over them and let them cook over a low heat for 25 minutes. Serve hot accompanied by fried potatoes.

Ingredients

Minced meat: beef and pork.
Tomatoes.
Onion.
Parsley.
Garlic.
An egg.
White wine.
Crumbled bread.
Pepper.
Flour.
Virgin olive oil.
Salt.

Kebabs

Chicken

Ingredients

Chicken off the bone.
Onion.
Garlic.
A bay leaf.
Black pepper.
White wine.
A vintage wine.
Chicken stock.
Virgin olive oil.
Salt.

Cut the chicken into small cubes, season to taste and put them on small wooden skewers. Fry in hot olive oil until they turn golden. Remove and set aside. In the same oil, sauté the onion and finely chopped garlic together with the bay leaf. When golden, add the white wine and the vintage wine and a little chicken stock. Thicken and blend. Serve with white rice, sprinkled with parsley and covered with the sauce.

Escalopes
withCheese

Ingredients

Fillets of beef/veal.
Cheese.
Fresh cream.
Brandy.
Butter.
An Egg.
Flour.
Breadcrumbs.
Virgin olive oil.
Salt.

Melt the cheese in a frying pan with butter over a low heat. Add the cream and a little brandy and reduce for 3 minutes before putting it in a mixer to make it creamier. Salt the fillets and turn them through the flour, beaten egg and breadcrumbs, in that order. Fry in hot oil. When serving, add the sauce and accompany with sliced and fried, or boiled potatoes.

57

Sirloin
withBoletusMushrooms

Soak the mushrooms in water for a quarter of an hour. Remove from water and fry gently in oil, as they tend to stick if the heat is high. Remove from heat and add cream, season to taste and return to a low heat for 10 minutes, adding some of the water used for soaking. Set aside. Cut the sirloin into thick slices, fry *au point* and season to taste.

Ingredients

Sirloin of pork or beef.
Boletus mushrooms.
Cream.
Pepper.
Virgin olive oil.
Salt.

Sirloin

withFoie

Ingredients

Sirloin of pork.
Duck liver pâté.
Red wine.
Pepper.
Virgin olive oil.
Salt.
Onion.
Carrots.
Leek.
Meat stock.
Flour.

Season the sirloin and cook it in a very hot frying pan with a drop of oil. Cut the pâté into slices and put them into a frying pan with a drizzle of oil. Let them cook in their own juice, turning them from side to side. Serve the sirloin alongside the pâté, covering everything with the sauce. To prepare the sauce, chop the onion, carrots and leek finely and sauté them in a frying pan. Add flour and let them toast on a low flame. Add the meat stock and stir. Let them cook and add salt. Crush the mixture and then sieve it, so as to acquire a smooth sauce.

Pork

Trotters

Ingredients

Pork trotters.
Tomatoes.
Onion. Garlic.
Paprika.
Ground pepper.
Bay leaf.
Parsley. Mint.
Saffron stems. Salt.

Clean the trotters and put them on the boil in a pot with the garlic, bay leaf, black pepper and plenty of salt. Meanwhile in a frying pan, fry the onion, tomatoes and garlic and add a teaspoonful of paprika at the end of the cooking process. Then add the now tender and strained trotters. Once fried, add the stock in which they were boiled. Add the parsley, a whole head of garlic and pepper, all of which have been previously crushed and simmer for 10 to 15 minutes. Serve with fried potatoes.

Cheek

ofBeef/Veal

Ingredients

Cheek of beef/veal.
Onion.
Carrot.
Leak.
Garlic.
Cloves.
Bay leaf.
Red wine.
Salt.
Pepper.

Brown the cheek in a casserole to seal it and set aside. Sauté the onion, carrot, leek, garlic, cloves and the bay leaf in the same oil. Season to taste and return the cheek to the mixture, adding red wine. Cover the casserole and cook for about 1 hour. Once cooked, separate the cheek from the vegetables, Crush the vegetables and then pass them through a food mill. The last step is to return the cheek to the sauce and check for salt. Serve with diced fried potatoes.

Tripe

Ingredients

Tripe.
Onion.
Garlic. Parsley.
Bay leaf.
Chilli.
White wine.
Cured ham.
Chorizo.
Sweet paprika.
Vinegar.
Virgin olive oil.
Salt.

Clean the tripe in lots of water. Put it to soak in salted water for an hour and then rinse it very well again. Chop up and boil in water for 5 minutes. Drain and place in a pot of cold water with a clove of garlic, chopped onion, parsley, the bay leaf and salt and leave to cook for 4 hours. Remove from the water and transfer to an earthenware casserole. Fry chopped onion and the chilli and once golden, add the diced cured ham and chorizo. Sauté, toss in a spoon of paprika and transfer to the casserole. In another pan, fry garlic and a bunch of parsley, then crush them and add to the other ingredients. Pour in glass of white wine and some of the water used for cooking. Bring to the boil and serve hot.

Potatoes

with Meat

Ingredients

Beef.
Potatoes.
Ripe tomato.
Onion.
Garlic.
White wine.
Bay leaf.
Yellow food colouring.
Nutmeg.
Rosemary.
Black pepper.
Virgin olive oil.
Salt.

Put 4 soupspoons of oil in a pan and fry the finely chopped onion and the garlic cut in thin slices. Meanwhile, cut the meat into cubes and set aside. Chop the tomato and add it to the onion and garlic and when cooked toss in the meat and let it brown a little. Add the wine, bay leaf, spices, colouring and salt and cook for 10 minutes, stirring from time to time to avoid the mixture sticking. Add the potatoes, cut into large pieces and cover with water. Cover the pot and cook till the meat and the potatoes are ready.

FriedChicken
withLemon

Ingredients

Chicken cut in small pieces.
Parsley.
Lemon
Garlic.
Virgin olive oil.
Salt.

Marinate the small pieces of chicken in sliced garlic and lemon juice. Leave for 2 hours. Separate the garlic from the marinade. Season the chicken pieces to taste and fry them in very hot oil until they are well browned. In the same frying pan and using part of the same oil, fry the garlic till it turns golden, together with the pieces of lemon. Once cooked, add the fried chicken and sprinkle with parsley.

Stuffed
Flamenquín

Ingredients

A fillet of pork tenderloin.

Cured ham.

Eggs.

Leak.

Garlic.

Tomato.

Boiled rice.

Flour.

Breadcrumbs.

Black pepper.

Salt.

Fry the leek, garlic, very finely chopped tomato and the boiled rice. Lay out the fillet, season to taste and place a slice of cured ham, a little hard-boiled egg and the fried ingredients on top of it. Roll it all up and secure it with a small wooden skewer, trying to ensure that the fried sauce won't come out when you fry it. Roll the *flamenquín* in flour, a beaten egg and breadcrumbs and fry it in oil that is not too strong. Serve with a little mayonnaise and accompany with marinated peppers, or a salad.

Braised Quail

Marinate the quail in brandy, cane syrup and thyme and leave to stand for 1 hour. Then season to taste and sauté in very hot oil until it browns. Remove the quail and sauté the onion, garlic, tomato, green pepper and aubergine in the same oil. Add the brandy and some stock and poach till cooked. Serve the quail with the vegetables. Additionally, it can also be served with small round potatoes.

Ingredients

A quail.
An Aubergine.
A Tomato.
A Green pepper.
Onion.
Garlic.
Brandy.
Thyme.
Cane syrup.
Virgin olive oil.
Salt.

Duck

withApple

Ingredients

A leg of confit de canard.
A pastry case.
An apple.
Sweet wine.
Fruits of the forest.
Onion.
Butter.
Black pepper.
Sugar.
Virgin olive oil.
Salt.

Break up the duck but keep the bone. Sauté the meat with the chopped onion and the sweet wine. Season to taste and place the ingredients in the centre of the pastry case. Close and place the bone in the centre of the parcel. Bake in the oven at 200°C for 8 minutes. Set aside. Peel the apple, dice it and sauté it in butter. Set aside. Sauté the fruits of the forest in butter and add some sweet wine, salt and sugar. Reduce. To serve, pour the fruity sauce into the middle of a plate, place the duck parcel on top and garnish with the apple.

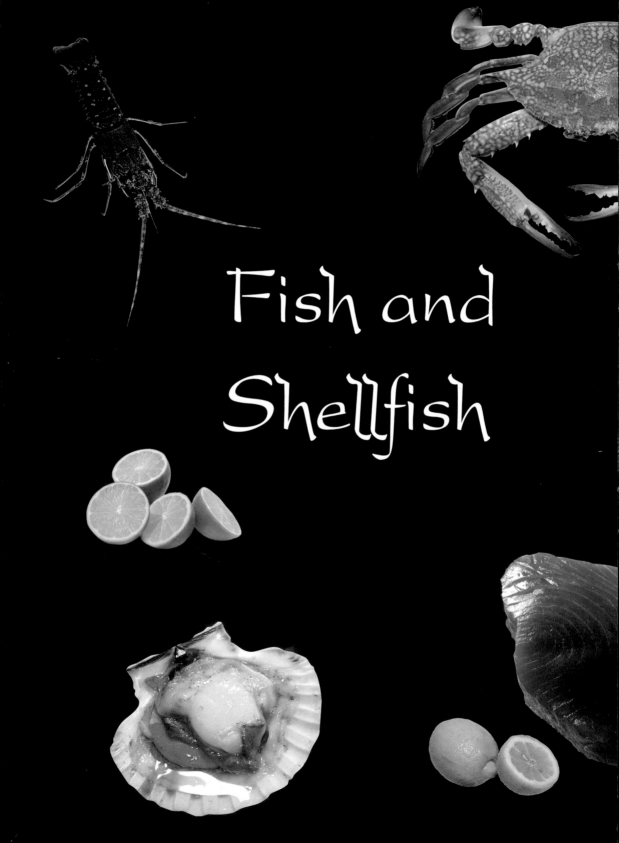

Fish and Shellfish

Fish are a source of vitamins and minerals, such as phosphorus, magnesium, selenium and iodine, above all those from the sea. These contain more sodium than those from fresh water and tinned, salted and smoked fish are those that have the most sodium. Fish meat has a very distinctive whitish colour, which is related to the colour of the blood, although there are also fish with red blood, such as the salmon. It is characterised by its large proportion of water compared to fat and for being very digestible. Seafood products are often the protagonists on menus for celebrations but there is no need why they shouldn't be part of an everyday diet. Freshness and quality are fundamental aspects to avoid intoxication. Shellfish is made up of molluscs (clams, mussels...) and crustaceans (Barnacles, prawns, lobster...) and has throughout history been of less importance than other animals, except in certain geographical areas, but is much appreciated today. Like fish, it provides a considerable amount of protein as well as calcium and iron. It also provides vitamins A, B2, B6 and B12. The fat content of shellfish is not very high, the most important being the Omega 3 fatty acids. It has long been known that people who consumed large quantities of seafood and shellfish had a low incidence of cardiovascular diseases; like the Eskimos for example. In order for it to be really good for us, we need to know what kind to buy and how to prepare it – roasted, stewed, fried, sautéed or boiled – all have their advantages.

KingPrawns
withRiceandAioli

Ingredients

King prawns.
Milk.
Onion.
Garlic.
Parsley.
Short-grained rice.
Sunflower oil.
Virgin olive oil.
Salt.

Peel the king prawns, leaving the tails on and set aside. To make the aioli, mix the milk, garlic and parsley with salt and beat. Then, stirring constantly, add the sunflower oil bit by bit until the sauce is thick. Place in the fridge. To prepare the rice, put some olive oil in a shallow pan and sweat half of the chopped onion. Then add the rice and salt and stir well cover the rice in oil. Add water bit by bit over a low heat. When the rice is al dente, remove from the heat and set aside 10 minutes. To finish, mix the rice with the aioli in a bowl suitable for a microwave and heat for about 1 minute. Meanwhile, in a preheated frying pan, sauté the king prawns. Serve the rice in the form of a volcano in the centre of a plate, with the prawns lying on the rice. Accompany with a little salsa verde or aioli, thinned with milk to make it more liquid.

Ingredients

A tube of clean squid.

Asparagus.

Bacon.

Onion.

A hard-boiled egg.

Parsley.

Gherkins.

Capers.

Anchovies.

Mayonnaise.

To make the tartar sauce, chop all the following ingredients finely: onion, egg, parsley, gherkins, capers and anchovies and mix with the mayonnaise. Set aside. To prepare the involtini, slice the squid lengthwise in fine less than 1cm thick strips. Then spread out the slices of bacon and over each one place half a strip of squid and an asparagus crosswise, then roll up the bacon to form the involtini. Put a few drops of oil in a non-stick frying pan, add the involtinis, and turn them for 1 minute on each side. Serve the involtinis on a base of tartar sauce on a plate. Decorate to taste.

SquidandAsparagus
Involtini(rolls)

Clams

alaMarinera

Ingredients

Clams.
Onion.
Parsley.
Bay leaf.
Sweet and hot paprika.
White wine.
Flour.
Virgin olive oil.
Salt.

Leave the clams for a few hours in a bowl of salted water so that they expel any sand. Sweat the previously finely chopped onion in olive oil in a frying pan over a high heat and then add the clams. When they begin to open, add the white wine, paprika, bay leaf, chopped parsley and finally the flour. Let everything boil for quite a while, stirring continuously, so that the sauce doesn't stick.

Stuffed

Wash the mussels well, scraping them with a knife to remove all traces of algae and dirt. Place the mussels in a pan, the bottom of which has been rubbed with garlic, adding half a cup of water. Cover and cook until they open. In another pan, sauté some chopped onion in oil and when it changes colour, add chopped cured ham and the chopped mussels. In a third pan, melt some butter, add flour and stirring with a wooden spoon, add the milk slowly. Salt to taste and cook for 10 minutes, stirring constantly. Fill each half-shell with the fried mixture, cover with béchamel and leave to cool. Coat with beaten egg and then breadcrumbs. Fry in plenty of hot oil and serve.

Ingredients

Mussels.
Onion.
Cured ham.
Flour.
Milk.
Eggs.
Breadcrumbs.
Virgin olive oil.
Salt.

Mussels

inVinaigrette

Wash and cook the mussels as above. Chop the tomatoes, pepper and onion very finely, season with oil, vinegar and salt and mix well. Open the mussels, remove half of the shell and discard. Place the remaining half with the mussel in a serving dish and dress with the vinaigrette.

Ingredients

Mussels.
Onion. Vinegar.
Green pepper.
Tomatoes. Salt.
Virgin olive oil.

Squid

Grilled

Clean the squid and brush them lightly with olive oil. On an iron (or electric) grilling plate, turn them on each side for a few minutes till they take on colour. Once ready, sprinkle them with salt and serve them on a plate, generously covering them with a sauce prepared from olive oil, lemon juice, finely chopped garlic and parsley. This sauce can be served either hot or cold. Alternatively they can be accompanied by aioli, tartar sauce, cocktail sauce, or simply mayonnaise.

Ingredients

Baby Squid.
Lemon.
Garlic.
Parsley.
Virgin olive oil.
Salt.

withOnions

Ingredients

Baby squid.
Onion.
Flour.
White wine.
Black pepper.
Garlic.
Parsley.
Fish stock.
Virgin olive oil.
Salt.

Clean the baby squid and leave them whole. In a pan, fry some julienned onion, black pepper corns and finely sliced garlic. When brown, added the flour and cook, adding white wine. Then quickly add the squid and let them cook very slowly. Once the wine reduces, add the fish stock. Check that they are tender and dress with parsley and the sauce you have prepared. Serve accompanied by fried or boiled potatoes, or white rice.

Prawns
Garlic

Ingredients

Prawns.
Garlic.
Chilli.
Parsley.
Virgin olive oil.
Salt.

Peel and chop the cloves of garlic, the chilli and the parsley. Peel the raw prawns without washing them. Put three tablespoons of oil in an earthenware dish and heat. When warm, add the chopped garlic, sauté for 1 minute and add the chilli. Then add the prawns, season to taste and sprinkle with a little chopped parsley. Finally, fry everything over a high heat for 4 minutes, shaking the dish occasionally.

withMushrooms

Heat some oil in a frying pan and toast the chilli and the garlic, both sliced finely. Add the mushrooms, stir, add salt and cook over a low heat 15 minutes, stirring occasionally. Then, add the prawns and chopped parsley, give the mixture and couple of stirs over a high flame and set aside as soon as the mixture changes colour, so as not to overcook. Serve hot.

in Vinegar

Ingredients

Fresh anchovies.
Vinegar.
Garlic.
Parsley.
Virgin olive oil.
Salt.

Clean the anchovies well and remove the tripe. Place them on a flat dish, cover with vinegar and salt and

leave to marinate 4 hours in the refrigerator. The action of the vinegar causes the anchovy to turn white. Peel and chop the garlic and parsley and mix with the oil. Remove the anchovies from the vinegar and place them in another flat dish, with the oil, garlic and parsley mixture. Before serving, leave to stand for about another hour, so that they absorb the flavour of the dressing.

Fresh Anchovies

Clean the anchovies, removing the heads and the tripe. Once drained, flour, season to taste and fry in abundant hot oil. Remove when golden brown and drain on kitchen paper.

Ingredients

Fresh anchovies.
Flour.
Virgin olive oil.
Salt.

Fried

Battered Dogfish

Ingredients

Dogfish.
Vinegar.
Paprika.
Oregano.
Cumin.
Flour.
Virgin olive oil.
Salt.

Cut the dogfish into 4 cm cubes. Prepare a marinade pounding in a mortar or grind up the paprika, oregano, cumin and salt. Put the fish in bowl and smear all over with this marinade, diluted with vinegar. Sprinkle with a lot of water and place in the refrigerator overnight. The following day, drain the fish well, roll the cubes in flour and fry in hot oil. Serve accompanied by a simple salad of onion, lettuce and tomato.

Fritters
Fish

Ingredients

Desalted cod or hake.
Virgin olive oil.
Sweet paprika.
Lemon.
Flour.
Egg.

Cut the fish into thick strips. Prepare a marinade with oil, paprika and the juice of one lemon. Add the pieces of fish, mix well and let stand for 1 hour, stirring occasionally. Remove from the marinade and drain in a colander. Roll each piece of fish in flour and beaten egg and fry in abundant very hot oil. Serve with a salad

Fried Bacalao

Ingredients

A fillet of cod.
Virgin olive oil.
Flour.

Desalt the cod, drain well, cut into cubes and flour. Fry in oil over a high heat until the batter turns a golden brown.

Hamburger

ofRedTuna

Ingredients

Red tuna.
Onion. Garlic.
Parsley. Salt.
Virgin olive oil.
Tabasco sauce.
Worcester Sauce.
Black pepper.
An avocado.
Tomato.
Soy sauce.
Lemon.
A sesame seed hamburger bun.
Antigua mustard.

To prepare the burger, put the tuna, onion, garlic and parsley in a shredder. Once chopped, add olive oil, Tabasco, Worcester sauce, salt and pepper and mix well. Divide the resulting mixture in four and shape in round steaks. Place in the fridge. To prepare the sauce, chop the avocado, parsley, onion and peeled and deseeded tomato. Dress with olive oil, soy sauce and lemon juice and mix well. In a pan, with a little hot oil, fry the burgers until cooked to taste. Serve on a plate with the two halves of the bun soft side up. Put the avocado sauce and the burger on the bottom half and sliced tomato and a little mustard on the top half.

Corvina

with Piquillo Peppers

Mix the oil, very finely chopped garlic and parsley, lemon juice and the juice from the peppers in a bowl and set aside for 1 hour. Salt the fish to taste and cook it on an iron grill until it is looks cooked to your taste. Remove and present in a dish garnished with the lemon, parsley and Piquillo peppers. Sprinkle with the reserved sauce and serve immediately, while hot.

Ingredients

Corvina (Meagre Fish).
Piquillo peppers.
Garlic.
Lemon.
Parsley.
Virgin olive oil.
Salt.

Octopus
Feira

High quality cooked octopus, whether fresh or frozen, is readily available on the market and will save us the trouble of having to scare and cook the animal. Heat the octopus over steam, cut into half-centimetre slices and place on a wooden board. Sprinkle with course salt, a mix of hot and sweet paprika and pour a generous quantity of olive oil over it. Serve with boiled potatoes.

Ingredients

Boiled octopus.
Potatoes.
Sweet and hot paprika.
Virgin olive oil.
Course sea salt.

Fritters Shrimp

Ingredients

Shrimps.
Flour.
Onion.
Parsley.
Virgin olive oil.
Salt.

Mix the flour with salt and water and beat vigorously until achieving a smooth liquid batter. Cut the onion very finely and add it to the batter, together with the raw shrimps, chopped parsley and the salt. Mix and set aside. Fry the fritters in hot oil, putting the paste in with a spoon. Remove from the oil and place on kitchen paper to drain, so they don't remain oily. Serve hot.

Calamares
alaRomana

Ingredients

Fresh squid.
Flour.
Egg.
Milk.
Bay leaf.
Virgin olive oil.
Salt.
Lemon.

Clean and cut the squid in rings. Add lemon juice, a splash of olive oil and the bay leaf. Set aside for 30 minutes. Separately, prepare the batter by mixing the egg yokes with the flour (reserve the whites), season to taste, adding a little milk and beating well. In another bowl, whisk the whites until stiff and slowly add them to the yoke mixture, taking care they don't shrink. When the 30-minute marinade is over, drain the squid rings well and add it to the batter mix. Fry in plentiful and very hot oil until they turn golden. Serve accompanied with lemon slices.

Scallop
auGratin

Ingredients

A Scallop.
Garlic.
Parsley.
Onion.
Breadcrumbs.
Nutmeg.
Pepper.
Virgin olive oil.
Salt.

Open the scallop by giving it a quick blast in the oven and then clean and remove the small dark muscle. Peel and finely chop the onion and garlic. Heat some oil in a frying pan and sweat them. Season the scallop, cover it with this mixture and sprinkle it with breadcrumbs, parsley and a pinch of nutmeg. Place in an ovenproof dish and bake at 190°C for 15 minutes. Serve very hot.

Marinated
Salmon

Ingredients

A fresh fillet of salmon.
Coarse salt.
Sugar.
Dill.

Clean off the fat and remove the bones by pressing with
a finger and extracting them with tweezers. Leave the
skin on and sprinkle with dill. Prepare the
marinade with salt and sugar, mixing
well. Put some of the marinade in a
large bowl and place the fish skin
side down. Cover completely with
the rest of the marinade, Cover
with transparent film and place a
weight on it. Refrigerate for 36-48
hours. The salt causes the salmon
to release water, which on mixing with
the sugar, creates a syrup that should be
removed. Halfway through the process, turn
the fish over. At the end of the marinating period, take the
fish out of the bowl and wash it under water to remove the
remains of the marinade. Dry well with kitchen paper and
store in an airtight container to avoid any humidity getting
in. When ready to serve, cut in thin slices and present on a
large piece of toasted bread (country loaf) with a drizzle of
olive oil, or accompany it with a tartar sauce.

And others

Having tried to create mini chefs out of

us through the different sections so far:

Something to Pick, Greens and

Vegetables, Eggs, Meats, Fish

and Shellfish, we now arrive at this final

section, where I have tried to put together other

Tapas, which were difficult to categorise. Hence,

the above rather ambiguous and not at all original title. Rice, a

basic ingredient not just of the eastern coast of Spain, is the main element

used to experiment with tastes and garnishes, although other ingredients

are important. Rice needs breadth and not height and an appropriately

sized container. The fresher and more natural the ingredients used are,

goes without saying, although the remains of other meals can help things

improve too. The oil, different types of rice, the burner and its intensity,

all contribute to raising a dish to the level of an art. Other end products,

such as ensaladillas (mayonnaise based vegetable salads), noodle

dishes, croquettes and snails... have their place in this section. Advice and

preparation are specified in the recipes. Finally, the many different forms

of soups and stews, commonly called "spoon dishes" in Spain, especially

those made from chickpeas, which originate in the Jewish *adafina* of the

XVth century, to which the Christians added bacon and other pork products.

There are succulent recipes to be found in all the regions, combining local

pulses with vegetables, meat and fish. Given the advances in technology

and in materials used, the everyday approach to these tapas can vary

considerably but one thing remains constant – the traditional earthenware

pot. Be sure to prepare and taste all these dishes but, above all, share them,

because if this book is to serve for anything, the object of this and the other

sections is to create art, companionship and enjoyment for others.

Ensaladilla
de Gambas

Ingredients

New potatoes.
Carrots.
Eggs.
Prawns.
Onion.
Mayonnaise.
Salt.

Boil the potatoes (well-washed but not peeled), carrots and eggs, in plenty of salted water. Once the potatoes and carrots are cold, cube them and put them in a bowl together with the chopped hard-boiled eggs and the peeled prawns, which have been previously boiled in water with a handful of coarse salt. Add the finely chopped onion and plenty of mayonnaise, mix and serve.

Ajoblanco
(WhiteGarlic)

Ingredients

Crumbled pieces of bread.
Peeled almonds.
Garlic.
Grapes.
Vinegar.
Virgin olive oil.
Salt.

Put the bread in water, soak it well and drain. Pound the bread, almonds and garlic in a mortar until the mixture is very fine and then add the oil bit by bit, as if you were making a mayonnaise. Then lighten the paste with water and vinegar till it turns into a creamy broth. To serve, garnish with peeled grapes, a little caviar and a few drops of oil.

A StewMeat

Ingredients

Boil the chickpeas with the beef, morcilla chorizo, chicken leg and the raw bacon. Remove the foam that starts to form on the surface with a slotted spoon. When it stops producing foam, add the pumpkin, the chopped green beans and the paprika and test for salt. Once all the ingredients are tender, remove from the heat and serve.

Chickpeas.
Pumpkin.
Green beans.
Chorizo.
Morcilla (Black pudding).
Beef.
A chicken leg.
Raw bacon.
Sweet paprika.
Sal.

A SmallRoll with «Pringá»

«Pringá» is a mixture of boiled beef, chicken, chorizo, morcilla and fresh bacon. Once cooked, remove the «pringá» from the pan, mix, chop and spread inside a small toasted roll. Serve with a glass of wine.

Croquettes
ofStew

Ingredients

Meat from the stew.
Onion.
Flour.
Milk.
Egg.
Butter.
Breadcrumbs.
Parsley.
Virgin olive oil.
Salt.

Chop the boiled beef, chicken, chorizo, morcilla and bacon. Put two tablespoons of oil and a tablespoon of butter in a large frying pan and slowly sweat the chopped onion. Once soft, add all the chopped meat, stir and keep adding flour slowly until you don't notice it anymore. Add the parsley and milk so as to cover the meat. Test for salt. The mixture is ready once it easily comes away from the pan. Place it on a dish and allow to cool. Once cold, shape it in small balls and roll them in flour, beaten egg and breadcrumbs (in that order) and fry in plenty of hot oil. When they turn golden brown, remove and serve.

Cabrillas

(OtalaLactea)

Ingredients

Milk or Spanish Snails
(escargots).
Pepper corns.
Ground pepper.
Vinegar.
Chilli.
Green Pepper.
Garlic.
Onion.
Tomatoes.
Salt.

Cleanse the snails by feeding them solely on flour for two days, till their excrement is white. Clean them thoroughly with plenty of cold water and soak them in water, course salt and vinegar for 2 hours, until they release all their mucus. Then wash them again several times, until the water remains clean and clear. The body of the snail should stick well out of the shell and in order to achieve this, they should be cooked over a slow heat for 10 to 15 minutes. Fry the garlic, onion, tomato and ground pepper. When the tomato and onion are soft, take them out and put them through a food mill or blender, so that the skins are no longer apparent. Pour the sauce over the snails in a bowl, mix well and then return to the heat, so that the sauce reduces and impregnates the snails. Cooking them slowly for 15 to 20 minutes should be enough.

Ingredients

Snails (small).
A head of garlic.
Onion.
Virgin olive oil.
Salt.
Muñequilla: coriander,
ginger, nutmeg, black
pepper, cloves, cinnamon,
cardamom, cayenne
pepper, cumin, oregano
and pennyroyal.

Cleanse the snails in a container with water for 24
hours to get rid of the slime. Then rinse them under
plenty of cold running water, changing them some
10 to 12 times. Once clean, put them in a tall pan,
covered with water and cover the pot. Cook on
a very low heat till they no longer stick to the pot.
Then raise the heat and skim until there is no more
foam. When the bodies come out of the shells, add
the muñequilla (bouquet garni) with all the herbs
(according to taste) tightly bound inside, so they
don't spill out, the squashed garlic head and salt.
They will be ready in 10 minutes. When serving, add
a small bunch of mint and a dash of oil.

Caracoles

Fideuá

(SeafoodStewwithNoodles)

withMushroomsand
CatalanSausage

withCuttlefishandPrawns

withBacalaoandRazorClams

alaMarinera

withChicken

withMeat

withVegetables

This dish, which originates from the coast of Valencia, is prepared in a similar way to paella. Hence it can be made with seafood, meat or vegetables. The secret is in making it crisp and in making sure the mixture of flavours is right. Different sizes of noodles can be used and may be accompanied only with lemon, or aioli or any sauce compatible with the ingredients used.

Grate the tomatoes and add a pinch of sugar to eliminate the acidity. Peel and chop the onion, peel the garlic and bash them, so they open. Chop up the squid and clean the king prawns. Preheat the oven and grill to 200°C. Put a good splash of olive oil in a paella pan, turn the king prawns back and forth with a little salt, remove from the heat and set aside. Add a little oil and sweat the onion with a pinch of salt over a low heat. Add the garlic cloves and let them release their aroma and flavour. Once the onion has sweated, add the squid, season to taste and let it release its water. Once it has evaporated, add the white wine, let it reduce and add the tomatoes, mixing well and allowing their water to evaporate. Then season with paprika, white pepper and saffron. Toast the spices for a moment and then add the noodles and toast them as well, stirring continuously. Add the fish stock and the peeled prawns. Raise the heat to maximum until the ingredients begin to boil, then lower it and allow the noodles to cook. One must put the *fideuá* in the oven before the liquid has been completely absorbed. If the paella dish is not suitable for the oven, reserve the prawns and put the noodles on a baking tray and bake till they are drier and start to stick up, which will take 10-15 minutes. Serve with aioli.

Ingredients

Noodles.
Squid.
King prawns.
Prawns.
Tomatoes.
Onion. Garlic.
White pepper.
Saffron.
Sweet paprika.
White wine.
Fish stock.
Virgin olive oil.
Salt. Sugar. Parsley.
Aioli.

Croquettes
Morcilla

Ingredients

Morcilla de Burgos
(A form of blood sausage).
Onion.
Butter.
Flour.
Chicken stock.
Milk.
Pine nuts.
Salt.

Sauté the onion in butter and once poached, add the *morcilla* and brown before adding the flour. Turn the resulting dough well and, once smooth, add the milk and hot broth taking care that no lumps appear and then, optionally, the pine nuts. Once the dough is ready and has cooled, form small balls, roll these in flour, beaten egg and breadcrumbs and fry in plenty of very hot oil. When browned, remove and serve with a salad.

Ravioli

Oxtail

Ingredients

Wanton pastry.
Stewed oxtail.
Potatoes.
Juices from the stewed oxtail.
Chives.
Sunflower oil.
Salt.

Place some shredded oxtail in the centre of a piece of Wanton pastry, moisten the edges with water and seal with another piece, to create the ravioli. Fry until crisp. Serve the ravioli on a base of diced fried potatoes and pour some of the previously heated oxtail stew juices over them. Garnish with chopped chives.

Crepe
VegetableandChicken

Ingredients

Buckwheat flour.
Milk.
Eggs.
Butter.
Chopped chicken.
Red and green pepper.
Caramelised onion.
Courgette.
Garlic.
Balsamic Vinegar.
Virgin olive oil.
Salt.

Place the flour in a bowl and gradually add the milk, eggs and salt and stir. The resulting batter must be smooth. Put aside for 20 minutes. Then spread a medium-sized frying pan with butter and heat over a medium flame. Pour in a little of the batter and cover the whole bottom of the pan. Once the underside of the crepe is browned, turn with a spatula and brown on the other side. Julienne the vegetables and poach them. Sauté the chicken and add it to the vegetables and caramelised onions. Fill the crepe and wrap it. To serve, garnish with a little Balsamic vinegar.

Croquettes

PorkCheek

Ingredients

Stewed Iberian pork cheeks.
Béchamel.
Japanese breadcrumbs "panko".
Virgin olive oil.

Prepare a traditional homemade béchamel. Add the stewed Iberian pork cheeks, or any other left over stewed meat. Once mixed, roll in Japanese "panko". Fry in abundant hot oil and serve with a garnish of mixed lettuces and tomato.

Fabada

Asturiana

Ingredients

White or Butter Beans.
Asturian chorizo.
Asturian morcilla.
Shoulder of pork.
Bacon (pork belly).
Garlic.
Virgin olive oil.
Salt.

Put the beans in plenty of water and leave to soak overnight. In a large pot, cover them with water and a little oil, heat and skim off the foam. Change the water and put in the chorizo, morcilla, shoulder of pork and bacon (compango). Depending on the quality of the bean, leave to cook over a low to medium heat for about 3 hours and cut the boil with cold water, 3 or 4 times. Season to taste at the end of the cooking process. If it remains a bit liquid, crush a few of the beans to thicken the sauce.

Lentils

with Vegetables

Wash, peel and chop the vegetables into small pieces, except for the celery that only lends aroma and flavour. Wash the lentils and put them in a pot with the vegetables, bay leaf, peeled garlic, a tablespoonful of sweet paprika and salt. Cover with water and a good splash of oil and bring to the boil. At this point, reduce the heat to a little more than minimum and simmer for 40 minutes, checking the salt. Before serving, remove the bunch of celery.

Ingredients

Lentils.
Potatoes.
Carrots.
A Courgette.
Leeks.
A green pepper.
Tomato.
A bunch of celery.
Garlic.
Sweet paprika.
A bay leaf.
Virgin olive oil.
Salt.

Aubergines
withSalmorejo

Ingredients

Aubergines.
Flour.
Virgin olive oil.
Salt.
Cream of salmorejo.

Cut the aubergines into sticks and season.
Mix flour with water to form a smooth batter.
Dip the aubergines in the batter and fry in
very hot oil. When golden brown, remove and
drain on kitchen paper. Serve accompanied
by a cream of salmorejo.

SanJacobo

Ingredients

Two fillets of beef.
Cured ham.
Cheese.
Flour.
Egg.
Breadcrumbs.
Pepper.
Virgin olive oil.
Salt.

Season the fillets and prepare the *San Jacobo,* which consists of one fillet, a slice of ham, another of cheese and the other fillet. Once prepared, turn in flour, beaten egg and breadcrumbs (in that order). Fry in abundant hot oil and remove once golden on both sides. Serve with vegetables and a little mayonnaise.

Paellas

of Seafood

Sauté the onion with the garlic and the peppers and then add the squid, the tomato and white wine. Cook for 20 minutes over a low heat. Add the rice and the stock, in which the saffron has been diluted. Cook for 10 minutes, add the seafood and peas. To finish the cooking, season with salt and add the previously boiled clams and mussels, the strips of roasted peppers and the chopped parsley. Turn off the heat and let the paella stand for a few minutes. Serve in the same pan, decorated with a few slices of lemon.

Ingredients

Rice.
Squid.
Mussels.
Clams.
Mantis shrimp.
Prawns.
Fish stock.
Peas.
Tomato.
Green and red peppers.
Saffron strands.
Garlic. Onion.
White wine.
Lemon. Parsley. Salt.
Virgin olive oil.

# of Vegetables

Ingredients

Rice.
Courgette.
Green beans. Peas.
Carrots.
Artichokes.
A Pepper. Tomatoes.
Ground pepper.
Onion. Garlic.
Saffron.
Vegetable Stock.
Olive oil. Salt.
White wine.

Heat oil in the paella pan and sauté the onion until transparent. Then add the vegetables, cut into cubes, and sauté everything for around 15 minutes. Add the rice and stir everything together. Add the crushed garlic, parsley and the saffron, diluted in a little water. Continuing to stir, add the stock, check for salt and cook until the rice is au point. Turn off the heat and always leave the paella to stand for a few minutes before serving.

# of Chicken

Fry the chicken pieces and set aside. Cut the green pepper, tomato, green beans, onion and garlic into cubes and fry. Once everything is sautéed, add the browned chicken and the rice, stir everything together and add the lemon juice, ground pepper, saffron, rosemary, thyme, salt and chicken stock, in proportion to the rice used. At first, place over a high flame and halfway through the cooking, reduce to medium. After about 20 minutes, it will be ready to serve, which includes the resting period.

Ingredients

Rice.
Chopped chicken.
A Pepper. Tomato.
Green beans.
Ground pepper.
Onion. Garlic. Parsley.
Rosemary. Thyme. Saffron.
Virgin olive oil. Salt.
Chicken stock. Lemon.

Tapas
from the Spanish kitchen

was printed in Seville
on the 21st of April 2011.

Breads

ROSEMARY BREAD TRIOS

Preparation time: 40 minutes + 1 hour 30 minutes rising
Total cooking time: 15 minutes
Makes 10 trios

7 g (¹/₄ oz) sachet dried yeast
1 teaspoon caster sugar
4 cups (500 g/1 lb) plain flour
1 tablespoon caster sugar, extra
1 teaspoon salt
1 cup (250 ml/8 fl oz) warm milk
¹/₄ cup (60 ml/2 fl oz) vegetable oil
10 small sprigs of rosemary
1 egg yolk
sea salt flakes, to sprinkle

1 Combine the yeast, caster sugar and ¹/₂ cup (125 ml/4 fl oz) of warm water in a small bowl. Cover and set aside in a warm place for 10 minutes, or until frothy.

2 Sift the flour into a large bowl and stir in the extra caster sugar and salt. Make a well in the centre and pour in the warm milk, oil and frothy yeast. Mix to a soft dough, gather into a ball then turn out onto a lightly floured surface and knead for 10 minutes, or until smooth and elastic. Add a little extra flour if the dough becomes too sticky. Place in a large, oiled bowl, cover loosely with greased plastic wrap and leave in a warm place for 1 hour, or until doubled in size.

3 Punch down the dough, then turn out onto a lightly floured surface and knead for 1 minute. Lightly grease 2 large baking trays. Divide the dough into 10 pieces. Form each piece into three balls—keeping the remaining pieces covered—and place close together on the prepared baking tray; add a sprig of rosemary to the centre of each trio. Repeat with the remaining pieces of dough, and lay each set separately on the baking tray.

4 Cover the trios with a damp tea towel and set aside for 20 minutes, or until well risen. Preheat the oven to moderate 180°C (350°F/Gas 4). Brush the trios lightly with the combined egg yolk and 1 teaspoon of water and sprinkle with the sea salt flakes. Bake for 15 minutes, or until golden brown. Allow to cool on a wire rack and replace the rosemary sprigs with fresh ones, if you want.

NUTRITION PER TRIO
Protein 7 g; Fat 8 g; Carbohydrate 40 g; Dietary Fibre 2 g; Cholesterol 20 mg; 1080 kJ (260 cal)

NOTE: 'Punching down' is when you knock the dough with your fist to expel the air.

Arrange the trio of balls together on a lightly greased baking tray.

Sprinkle the prosciutto and Parmesan on the dough, leaving a clear border.

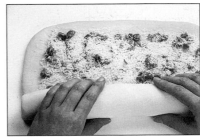

Roll up the dough tightly lengthways into a log shape for baking.

PARMESAN AND PROSCIUTTO LOAF

Preparation time: 30 minutes + 2 hours rising
Total cooking time: 25 minutes
Serves 6

7 g (¼ oz) dried yeast
1 teaspoon caster sugar
½ cup (125 ml/4 fl oz) warm milk
2 cups (250 g/8 oz) plain flour
1 teaspoon salt
1 egg, lightly beaten
30 g (1 oz) butter, melted and cooled slightly
1 tablespoon milk, extra
60 g (2 oz) sliced prosciutto, finely chopped
½ cup (50 g/1¾ oz) grated Parmesan

1 Mix the yeast, sugar and milk in a bowl. Cover and set aside in a warm place for 10 minutes, or until frothy.

2 Mix the flour and salt in a bowl. Make a well in the centre and add the egg, butter and frothy yeast. Mix to a soft dough and gather into a ball; turn out onto a floured surface and knead for 8 minutes, or until elastic.

3 Put in an oiled bowl, cover loosely with greased plastic wrap and leave in a warm place for 1¼ hours, or until doubled in size.

4 Punch down the dough, turn out onto a floured surface and knead for 30 seconds, or until smooth. Roll out to a rectangle, 30 x 20 cm (12 x 8 inches), and brush with some extra milk. Sprinkle with the prosciutto and Parmesan, leaving a border. Roll lengthways into a log shape.

5 Lay on a greased baking tray and brush with the remaining milk. Slash the loaf at intervals. Leave to rise in a warm place for 30 minutes. Bake at 220°C (425°F/Gas 7) for 25 minutes.

NUTRITION PER SERVE
Protein 10 g; Fat 9 g; Carbohydrate 30 g; Dietary Fibre 2 g; Cholesterol 60 mg; 1060 kJ (250 cal)

Spread the rectangle of dough with olive paste and roll up lengthways.

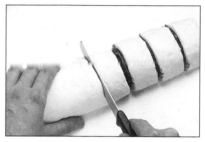

Using a serrated knife, cut the rolled log into 12 equal slices.

OLIVE SPIRALS

Preparation time: 25 minutes + 1 hour 40 minutes rising
Total cooking time: 35 minutes
Makes 12 spirals

7 g (¼ oz) dried yeast
1 teaspoon sugar
4 cups (500 g/1 lb) plain flour
1 teaspoon salt
2 tablespoons olive oil
2 cups (250 g/8 oz) pitted black olives
½ cup (50 g/1¾ oz) finely grated Parmesan
3 cloves garlic, chopped
1 tablespoon oil

1 Mix the yeast, sugar and ½ cup (125 ml/4 fl oz) warm water in a bowl. Cover and set aside in a warm place for 10 minutes, or until frothy.
2 Sift the flour and salt into a bowl and make a well in the centre. Add the frothy yeast, oil and 1 cup (250 ml/ 8 fl oz) of warm water. Mix to a soft dough and gather into a ball. Turn out onto a floured surface and knead for 10 minutes, or until smooth. Cover loosely with greased plastic wrap and set aside for 1 hour, or until well risen.
3 Process the olives, Parmesan and garlic in a food processor until chopped. With the motor running, add the tablespoon of oil and process to a paste.
4 Punch down the dough and knead for 1 minute. Roll out to a rectangle 42 x 35 cm (18 x 14 inches). Spread with the olive paste, leaving a border along one long side. Roll up length-ways, ending with the clear long side.

5 Cut into 12 slices and place close together on a greased baking tray. Cover with a damp tea towel and set aside for 30 minutes, or until well risen. Preheat the oven to moderately hot 200°C (400°F/Gas 6). Bake for 35 minutes, or until golden brown.

NUTRITION PER SPIRAL
Protein 8 g; Fat 8 g; Carbohydrate 40 g; Dietary Fibre 3 g; Cholesterol 4 mg; 1050 kJ (250 cal)

Spoon the filling onto one disc and top with another, pressing down firmly.

Stand the discs upright in the loaf tin, squashing them together.

CHEESE AND HERB PULL-APART LOAF

Preparation time: 25 minutes + 1 hour 40 minutes rising
Total cooking time: 30 minutes
Serves 8

7 g (¹/₄ oz) dried yeast
1 teaspoon sugar
4 cups (500 g/1 lb) plain flour
1¹/₂ teaspoons salt
2 tablespoons chopped fresh parsley
2 tablespoons chopped chives
1 tablespoon chopped fresh thyme
60 g (2 oz) Cheddar cheese, grated
milk, to glaze

1 Combine the yeast, sugar and ¹/₂ cup (125 ml/4 fl oz) of warm water in a small bowl. Cover and set aside in a warm place for 10 minutes, or until frothy.
2 Sift the flour and salt into a bowl. Make a well in the centre and pour in 1 cup (250 ml/8 fl oz) warm water and the frothy yeast. Mix to a soft dough. Knead on a lightly floured surface for 10 minutes, or until smooth. Put the dough in an oiled bowl, cover loosely with greased plastic wrap and leave for 1 hour, or until doubled in size.
3 Punch down and knead for 1 minute. Divide the dough in half and shape each half into 10 flat discs, 6 cm (2¹/₂ inches) in diameter. Mix the fresh herbs with the Cheddar and put 2 teaspoons on a disc. Press another disc on top. Repeat with the remaining discs and herb mixture.

4 Grease a 21 x 10.5 x 6.5 cm (8¹/₂ x 4¹/₄ x 2¹/₂ inch) loaf tin. Stand the filled discs upright in the prepared tin, squashing them together. Cover the tin with a damp tea towel and set aside in a warm place for 30 minutes, or until well risen. Preheat the oven to hot 210°C (415°F/Gas 6–7).
5 Glaze with a little milk and bake for 30 minutes, or until brown and crusty.

NUTRITION PER SERVE
Protein 10 g; Fat 4 g; Carbohydrate 60 g; Dietary Fibre 3 g; Cholesterol 8 mg; 1255 kJ (300 cal)

Brush the edge with the beaten egg and roll over to enclose the filling.

Plait the pieces together and place seam-side-down on a baking tray.

CARAMELIZED ONION BRAIDS

Preparation time: 1 hour + 1 hour 45 minutes rising
Total cooking time: 1 hour 35 minutes
Serves 10

2¹/₂ cups (310 g/10 oz) plain flour
1 cup (125 g/4 oz) buckwheat flour
1 teaspoon salt
15 g (¹/₂ oz) fresh yeast or 7 g (¹/₄ oz) dried yeast
1¹/₄ cups (315 ml/10 fl oz) warm milk
30 g (1 oz) butter
1 tablespoon oil
1 kg (2 lb) onions, thinly sliced into rings
1 egg, lightly beaten
2 teaspoons fennel seeds

1 Sift the flours and salt into a large bowl and make a well in the centre. Dissolve the yeast in ¹/₂ cup (125 ml/4 fl oz) of the warm milk in a small bowl. Then add the remaining warm milk. Pour into the well and mix to a dough. Turn out onto a floured surface and knead for 8 minutes, or until smooth. Place in a large oiled bowl, cover loosely with greased plastic wrap and leave in a warm place for 45 minutes–1 hour, or until doubled in size.

2 Melt the butter and oil in a frying pan, add the onion and cook over medium-low heat for 40–50 minutes, or until the onion is golden.

3 Punch down the dough, turn out onto a lightly floured surface and knead for 10 minutes, or until smooth and elastic.

4 Lightly grease 2 baking trays. Divide the dough in half. Working with 1 piece at a time, divide it into 3 pieces. Roll each piece out to a 30 x 10 cm (12 x 4 inch) rectangle. Divide the onion mixture into 6 portions and spread a portion along the middle of each rectangle, leaving a 2 cm (³/₄ inch) border. Brush the edge

with some of the beaten egg and roll over lengthways to enclose the filling.

5 Plait the 3 pieces together and place seam-side-down on a baking tray. Pinch the ends together. Repeat with the remaining dough and caramelized onion. Cover with a damp tea towel and leave in a warm place for 45 minutes, or until well risen.

6 Preheat the oven to moderate 180°C (350°F/Gas 4). Brush the top with the beaten egg and sprinkle with the fennel seeds. Bake for 35–45 minutes, or until well browned. Transfer to a wire rack to cool.

NUTRITION PER SERVE
Protein 8 g; Fat 7 g; Carbohydrate 40 g; Dietary Fibre 3 g; Cholesterol 30 mg; 1030 kJ (250 cal)

Make a well in the centre of the dry ingredients and add the herbs and beer.

Cook the loaf until it is well browned, then turn out onto a wire rack to cool.

BEER BREAD WITH SUN-DRIED TOMATO AND HERBS

Preparation time: 20 minutes
Total cooking time: 45 minutes
Serves 8

1 tablespoon finely chopped fresh oregano,
    or 1½ teaspoons dried
3 tablespoons finely chopped fresh parsley
2 tablespoons finely chopped fresh basil
3 tablespoons chopped sun-dried tomato
1 teaspoon cracked black pepper
3 tablespoons grated Parmesan
2 cloves garlic, crushed
3 cups (375 g/12 oz) self-raising flour
1 teaspoon salt
2 teaspoons sugar
1½ cups (375 ml/12 fl oz) beer (not bitter),
    at room temperature
2 teaspoons olive oil

1 Preheat the oven to 210°C (415°C/ Gas 6–7). Brush a 25 x 15 cm (10 x 6 inch) loaf tin with melted butter. Mix the oregano, parsley, basil, sun-dried tomato, pepper, cheese and garlic.
2 Sift the flour, salt and sugar into a large mixing bowl. Make a well in the centre and add the herb mixture and beer. Stir with a wooden spoon for 1 minute. (It should be very moist—add a little more beer if necessary.)
3 Spoon into the tin and smooth the surface. Bake for 10 minutes, then reduce to 180°C (350°F/Gas 4) and bake for 30 more minutes. Brush the top with oil and cook for 5 more minutes or until well browned and cooked through. Turn out onto a wire rack to cool.

NUTRITION PER SERVE
Protein 7 g; Fat 3 g; Carbohydrate 45 g; Dietary Fibre 2 g; Cholesterol 4 mg; 800 kJ (210 cal)

Make a well in the centre of the flour and then add the milk and vinegar mixture.

Mark the loaf into 8 wedges, cutting lightly into the top with a knife.

LEMON PEPPER DAMPER

Preparation time: 18 minutes
Total cooking time: 25 minutes
Serves 8

2 cups (250 g/8 oz) self-raising flour
1 teaspoon salt (see NOTE)
2 teaspoons lemon pepper, or 1 teaspoon
    grated lemon rind and 2 teaspoons black
    pepper
45 g (1½ oz) butter, chopped
1 tablespoon snipped chives
90 g (3 oz) Cheddar cheese, grated
2 teaspoons white vinegar
¾ cup (185 ml/6 fl oz) milk

1 Preheat the oven to 210°C (415°F/ Gas 6–7). Brush a baking tray with melted butter or oil. Sift the flour into a large bowl and add the salt and lemon pepper. Rub in the butter with your fingertips until the mixture resembles coarse breadcrumbs. Stir in the chives and grated cheese.

2 Stir the vinegar into the milk (it should look slightly curdled). Make a well in the middle of the flour, add the milk and mix to a soft dough, adding a little more milk if the dough is too stiff.

3 Turn out onto a lightly floured surface and knead until smooth. Place on the baking tray and press out into a circle approximately 2.5 cm (1 inch) thick. Mark with a knife into 8 wedges, cutting lightly into the top of damper. Dust the top lightly with flour. Bake for 25 minutes, or until the damper is deep golden and sounds hollow when tapped on the base.

NUTRITION PER SERVE
Protein 10 g; Fat 14 g; Carbohydrate 26 g; Dietary Fibre 1 g; Cholesterol 41 mg; 1118 kJ (267 cal)

NOTE: If you are using commercial lemon pepper, omit the salt.

On a lightly floured surface, knead the dough until it is smooth.

Knead the dough for 5 minutes, then add the capsicum and knead for another 5 minutes.

ROASTED RED CAPSICUM BUNS

Preparation time: 40 minutes + 1 hour 40 minutes rising
Total cooking time: 1 hour
Makes 8 buns

2 red capsicums, cut into large flat pieces
7 g (¼ oz) dried yeast
2 teaspoons sugar
4 cups (500 g/1 lb) plain flour
1 teaspoon salt
1 tablespoon olive oil
1 egg, lightly beaten

1 Place the capsicum skin-side-up under a hot grill, until the skins blacken. Cool in a plastic bag, then peel away the skin and dice the flesh.
2 Combine the dried yeast, sugar and ½ cup (125 ml/4 fl oz) of warm water in a bowl and leave in a warm place for 10 minutes, or until frothy.
3 Sift the flour and salt into a bowl, make a well in the centre and pour in the oil, the frothy yeast and 1¼ cups (315 ml/10 fl oz) of warm water. Mix to a soft dough, gather into a ball and knead on a floured surface until smooth. Add a little extra flour if needed. Place in a lightly oiled bowl, cover loosely with greased plastic wrap and leave in a warm place for 1 hour, or until doubled.

4 Punch down the dough, turn out onto a floured surface and knead for 10 minutes, adding the capsicum half-way through. Divide the dough into eight and form into rounds. Lay apart on a greased baking tray. Cover with a damp tea towel and leave for 30 minutes, or until well risen. Preheat the oven to 180°C (350°F/Gas 4). Brush the buns with beaten egg. Bake for 40–45 minutes, or until the bases sound hollow when tapped.

NUTRITION PER BUN
Protein 9 g; Fat 4 g; Carbohydrate 50 g; Dietary Fibre 3 g; Cholesterol 20 mg; 1125 kJ (270 cal)

Using a sharp floured knife, divide the dough into 12 equal portions.

The rolls are cooked when the bases sound hollow when tapped.

TOMATO HERB ROLLS

Preparation time: 30 minutes + 1 hour 25 minutes rising
Total cooking time: 35 minutes
Makes 12 rolls

7 g (¼ oz) dried yeast
1 teaspoon sugar
4 cups (500 g/l lb) plain flour
1 teaspoon salt
2 cloves garlic, finely chopped
½ cup (75 g/2½ oz) sun-dried tomatoes, finely chopped
1 tablespoon chopped fresh oregano
1 tablespoon chopped fresh marjoram
1 tablespoon chopped fresh thyme
2 tablespoons chopped fresh flat-leaf parsley
30 g (1 oz) butter, melted
½ cup (125 ml/4 fl oz) milk, plus extra, to glaze

1 Mix the yeast, sugar and ½ cup (125 ml/4 fl oz) of warm water in a bowl. Set aside for 10 minutes, or until frothy. Sift the flour and salt into a bowl and make a well in the centre.
2 Mix in the garlic, sun-dried tomato and herbs. Pour in the melted butter, frothy yeast and milk and mix to a soft dough. Knead on a lightly floured surface for 10 minutes, or until smooth. Cover loosely with greased plastic wrap and leave for 45 minutes, or until well risen.
3 Punch down and knead for 5 minutes. Divide into twelve and roll into balls. Lay apart on a greased baking tray. Leave for 30 minutes, or until well risen. Preheat the oven to hot 210°C (415°F/Gas 6–7). Brush the rolls with milk and bake for 10 minutes. Reduce the oven to 180°C (350°F/Gas 4) and bake for 20–25 minutes, or until golden.

NUTRITION PER ROLL
Protein 5 g; Fat 3 g; Carbohydrate 30 g; Dietary Fibre 2 g; Cholesterol 8 mg; 730 kJ (175 cal)

Dips

HUMMUS

Preparation time: 20 minutes + overnight soaking
Total cooking time: 1 hour 15 minutes
Serves 20

1 cup (220 g/7 oz) dried chickpeas
2 tablespoons tahini (sesame paste)
4 cloves garlic, crushed
2 teaspoons ground cumin
1/3 cup (80 ml/2 3/4 fl oz) lemon juice
3 tablespoons olive oil
large pinch cayenne pepper
extra lemon juice, optional
extra olive oil, to garnish
paprika, to garnish
chopped fresh parsley, to garnish

1 Soak the chickpeas in 1 litre water overnight. Drain and place in a large saucepan with 2 litres fresh water (enough to cover the chickpeas by 5 cm/2 inches). Bring to the boil, then reduce the heat and simmer for 1 hour 15 minutes, or until the chickpeas are very tender. Skim any froth from the surface. Drain well, reserve the cooking liquid and leave until cool enough to handle. Pick over for any loose skins and discard.

2 Process the chickpeas, tahini, garlic, cumin, lemon juice, olive oil, cayenne pepper and 1 1/2 teaspoons salt in a food processor until thick and smooth. With the motor still running, gradually add about 3/4 cup (185 ml/6 fl oz) reserved cooking liquid to form a smooth creamy purée. Season with salt or extra lemon juice.

3 Spread onto a flat bowl or plate, drizzle with oil, sprinkle with paprika and scatter the parsley over the top. Serve with pitta or pide breads that have been warmed on the barbecue.

NUTRITION PER SERVE

Protein 1.2 g; Fat 4.7 g; Carbohydrate 1.6 g; Dietary Fibre 0.9 g; Cholesterol 0 mg; 228 kJ (54 cal)

Pick through the cooled chickpeas to remove any loose skins.

Process the chickpea mixture with the reserved cooking liquid until creamy.

Remove the avocado stone by chopping into it with a sharp knife and lifting up.

You will only need a couple of drops of Tabasco or habanero—they are very hot.

GUACAMOLE

Preparation time: 30 minutes
Total cooking time: Nil
Serves 6

3 ripe avocados
1 tablespoon lime or lemon juice (see HINT)
1 tomato
1–2 red chillies, finely chopped
1 small red onion, finely chopped
1 tablespoon finely chopped fresh coriander
    leaves
2 tablespoons sour cream
1–2 drops Tabasco or habanero sauce

1 Roughly chop the avocado flesh and place in a bowl. Mash lightly with a fork and sprinkle with the lime or lemon juice to prevent the avocado discoloring.
2 Cut the tomato in half horizontally and use a teaspoon to scoop out the seeds. Finely dice the flesh and add to the avocado.
3 Stir in the chilli, onion, coriander, sour cream and Tabasco or habanero sauce. Season with freshly cracked black pepper.
4 Serve immediately or cover the surface with plastic wrap and refrigerate for 1–2 hours. If refrigerated, allow to come to room temperature before serving.

NUTRITION PER SERVE
Protein 3 g; Fat 30 g; Carbohydrate 2 g; Dietary Fibre 3 g; Cholesterol 9 mg; 1200 kJ (290 cal)

HINT: You will need 1–2 limes to produce 1 tablespoon of juice, depending on the lime. A heavier lime will probably be more juicy. To get more juice from a citrus fruit, prick it all over with a fork and then heat on High (100%) in the microwave for 1 minute. Don't forget to prick it or the fruit may burst.

Finely grate the rind and squeeze the juice from the fresh limes.

Mix together all the ingredients and leave in the fridge for 2 hours before serving.

PRAWN, CORN AND SWEET CHILLI DIP

Preparation time: 1 hour + 2 hours refrigeration
Total cooking time: 5 minutes
Serves 8

1 kg (2 lb) cooked prawns
juice and grated rind of 3 limes
100 g (3½ oz) frozen corn kernels
250 g (8 oz) soft cream cheese
¼ cup (15 g/½ oz) finely chopped chives
1 tablespoon sweet chilli sauce
4 cooked king prawns, to garnish

1 Peel, devein and rinse the prawns; pat them dry and place in a bowl. Add the lime juice to the prawns, cover and refrigerate for 10 minutes.
2 Cook the frozen corn kernels in boiling water for 2–3 minutes, or until tender. Drain and plunge the kernels into iced water to prevent further cooking, then drain and pat dry with paper towel.
3 Place the prawns and lime juice in a food processor and process in short bursts for 2–3 seconds until the prawns are chopped into small pieces but not minced.
4 Transfer the chopped prawns to a bowl and mix in the cream cheese, corn kernels, lime rind and chives. Add the chilli sauce and mix well. Cover the dip with plastic wrap and refrigerate for at least 2 hours. Just before serving, peel and devein the king prawns, leaving the tails intact. Transfer the dip to a serving bowl and garnish with the peeled prawns. Delicious served with a bowl of barbecued king prawns, for dipping.

NUTRITION PER SERVE
Protein 35 g; Fat 12 g; Carbohydrate 5 g; Dietary Fibre 0 g; Cholesterol 280 mg; 1090 kJ (260 cal)

Press the soaked bread pieces in a strainer to extract any excess milk.

Process the bread, tarama, egg yolk, onion and garlic until smooth.

TARAMASALATA

Preparation time: 10 minutes + 10 minutes soaking
Total cooking time: Nil
Serves 10

5 slices white bread, crusts removed
1/3 cup (80 ml/2¾ fl oz) milk
100 g (3½ oz) can tarama (mullet roe)
1 egg yolk
½ small onion, grated
1 clove garlic, crushed
2 tablespoons lemon juice
1/3 cup (80 ml/2¾ fl oz) olive oil
pinch ground white pepper

1 Soak the bread in the milk for 10 minutes. Press in a strainer to extract any excess milk, then place in a food processor with the tarama, egg yolk, onion and garlic. Process for 30 seconds, or until smooth, then add 1 tablespoon lemon juice.

2 With the motor running, slowly pour in the olive oil. The mixture should be smooth and of a dipping consistency. Add the remaining lemon juice and a pinch of white pepper. If too salty, add another piece of bread.

NUTRITION PER SERVE
Protein 3.8 g; Fat 10.4 g; Carbohydrate 8.3 g; Dietary Fibre 0.6 g; Cholesterol 57 mg; 596 kJ (142 cal)

VARIATION: Try smoked cod's roe instead of the mullet roe.

Stir the lemon juice into the thick and creamy mayonnaise.

Refresh the asparagus spears by plunging into a bowl of iced water.

GARLIC DIP WITH CRUDITES

Preparation time: 15 minutes
Total cooking time: 15 minutes
Serves 4

4 cloves garlic, crushed
2 egg yolks
300 ml (10 fl oz) light olive or vegetable oil
1 tablespoon lemon juice
pinch ground white pepper
12 asparagus spears, trimmed
26 radishes, trimmed
1/2 telegraph cucumber, seeded, halved and cut into batons
1 head witlof, leaves separated

1 Place the garlic, egg yolks and a pinch of salt in the bowl of a food processor. Process for 10 seconds.

2 With the motor running, add the oil in a thin, slow stream. The mixture will start to thicken. When this happens you can add the oil a little faster. Process until all the oil is incorporated and the mayonnaise is thick and creamy. Transfer to a bowl and stir in the lemon juice and a pinch of pepper.

3 Bring a saucepan of water to the boil, add the asparagus and cook for 1 minute. Remove and plunge into a bowl of iced water. Arrange the asparagus, radish, cucumber and witlof on a platter and place the garlic dip in a bowl on the platter.

NUTRITION PER SERVE
Protein 3 g; Fat 74 g; Carbohydrate 1.5 g; Dietary Fibre 2 g; Cholesterol 90 mg; 28807 kJ (670 cal)

NOTE: Should the mayonnaise start to curdle as the oil is added, beat in 1–2 teaspoons boiling water. If this fails, put another egg yolk in a clean bowl and very slowly whisk in the curdled mixture, one drop at a time, then continue as above.

HINT: For best results when making mayonnaise, make sure all the ingredients are at room temperature before you start.

Soak the bread in the milk for 2 minutes, then mash up with your fingertips.

Add the spring onion, yoghurt, herbs, oil, lemon juice, rind and seasoning.

WHITE BEAN, CHICKPEA AND HERB DIP

Preparation time: 20 minutes + overnight soaking
Total cooking time: 1 hour
Serves 12

180 g (6 oz) dried cannellini beans
100 g (3½ oz) dried chickpeas
3 slices white bread
3 tablespoons milk
2 spring onions, finely chopped
4 tablespoons thick plain yoghurt
1 tablespoon lemon juice
2 teaspoons finely grated lemon rind
1 tablespoon chopped fresh parsley
2 teaspoons chopped fresh oregano
2 tablespoons olive oil

1 Soak the beans and chickpeas in cold water overnight. Rinse well and transfer to a pan. Cover with cold water and bring to the boil. Reduce the heat and simmer for 1 hour, or until very tender, adding more water if needed. Skim any froth from the surface. Drain well, cool and mash.

2 Remove the crusts from the bread, place in a bowl and drizzle with the milk. Leave for 2 minutes, then mash with your fingertips until very soft. Mix together with the beans.

3 Add the spring onion, yoghurt, lemon juice, rind, fresh herbs and oil and season well. Mix together well and serve at room temperature.

NUTRITION PER SERVE
Protein 4 g; Fat 4 g; Carbohydrate 12 g; Dietary Fibre 2 g; Cholesterol 2 mg; 416 kJ (99 cal)

Mix the yoghurt, crushed garlic, mint and lemon juice together.

Squeeze the grated cucumber to remove any excess moisture.

TZATZIKI

Preparation time: 10 minutes + 15 minutes standing
Total cooking time: Nil
Serves 12

2 Lebanese cucumbers
400 g (13 oz) Greek-style plain yoghurt
4 cloves garlic, crushed
3 tablespoons finely chopped fresh mint, plus extra to garnish
1 tablespoon lemon juice

1 Cut the cucumbers in half lengthways, scoop out the seeds and discard. Leave the skin on and coarsely grate the cucumber into a small colander. Sprinkle with salt and leave over a large bowl for 15 minutes to drain off any bitter juices.
2 Meanwhile, stir together the yoghurt, crushed garlic, mint and lemon juice.
3 Rinse the cucumber under cold water then, taking small handfuls, squeeze out any excess moisture. Combine the grated cucumber with the yoghurt mixture and season well. Serve immediately with pitta or pide bread or as a sauce with chicken.

NUTRITION PER SERVE
Protein 1.6 g; Fat 1.2 g; Carbohydrate 2.3 g; Dietary Fibre 0.5 g; Cholesterol 5.3 mg; 119 kJ (28 cal)

STORAGE: Will keep in an airtight container in the fridge for 2–3 days.

Use an olive pitter or small sharp knife to remove the stones from the olives.

Process all the ingredients in a food processor until smooth.

TAPENADE

Preparation time: 10 minutes
Total cooking time: Nil
Serves 10

400 g (13 oz) Kalamata olives, pitted
2 cloves garlic, crushed
2 anchovy fillets in oil, drained
2 tablespoons capers in brine, rinsed,
    squeezed dry
2 teaspoons chopped fresh thyme
2 teaspoons Dijon mustard
1 tablespoon lemon juice
3 tablespoons olive oil
1 tablespoon brandy, optional

1 Place the kalamata olives, crushed garlic, anchovies, capers, chopped thyme, Dijon mustard, lemon juice, olive oil and brandy in a food processor and process until smooth. Season with salt and black pepper. Spoon into a clean, warm jar, cover with a layer of olive oil, seal and refrigerate for up to 1 week. Serve as a dip with bruschetta and olives.

NUTRITION PER SERVE
Protein 1.3 g; Fat 2.4 g; Carbohydrate 2 g; Dietary Fibre 8.5 g; Cholesterol 0.6 mg; 376 kJ (90 cal)

NOTE: When refrigerated, the olive oil may solidify, turning it opaque white. This is a property of olive oil and will not affect the flavor of the dish. Simply bring to room temperature before serving and the olive oil will return to a liquid state. The word 'tapenade' comes from the French word tapéno, meaning capers. Tapenade is the famous olive, anchovy and caper spread from Provence.

HINT: To make sure your storage jar is very clean, preheat the oven to very slow 120°C (250°F/Gas ¹/₂). Wash the jar and lid thoroughly in hot soapy water (or preferably in a dishwasher) and rinse well with hot water. Put the jar on a baking tray and place in the oven for 20 minutes, or until fully dry and you are ready to use it. Do not dry the jar or lid with a tea towel.

Process the pine nuts, basil, garlic, sea salt and oil until smooth.

Transfer to a bowl and stir the Parmesan and pecorino into the basil mixture.

PESTO

Preparation time: 10 minutes
Total cooking time: 5 minutes
Serves 6

50 g (1³/₄ oz) pine nuts
50 g (1³/₄ oz) small fresh basil leaves
2 cloves garlic, crushed
¹/₂ teaspoon sea salt
¹/₂ cup (125 ml/4 fl oz) olive oil
30 g (1 oz) Parmesan, finely grated
20 g (³/₄ oz) pecorino cheese, finely grated

1 Preheat the oven to 180°C (350°F/ Gas 4). Spread the pine nuts on a baking tray and bake for 2 minutes, or until lightly golden. Cool.
2 Chop the pine nuts, basil, garlic, salt and oil in a food processor until smooth. Transfer to a bowl and stir in the cheeses. Serve as a dip with bread, crackers or crudités, or as a sauce for barbecued meat, chicken or seafood.

NUTRITION PER SERVE
Protein 4 g; Fat 28 g; Carbohydrate 0.5 g; Dietary Fibre 0.6 g; Cholesterol 7.6 mg; 1118 kJ (267 cal)

Mix the chopped artichoke with the mayonnaise, Parmesan and onion flakes.

Spread the dip in a shallow dish and sprinkle with Parmesan and paprika.

ARTICHOKE DIP

Preparation time: 10 minutes
Total cooking time: 15 minutes
Serves 8

2 x 400 g (13 oz) cans artichoke hearts, drained
1 cup (250 g/8 oz) mayonnaise
³/₄ cup (75 g/2¹/₂ oz) grated Parmesan
2 teaspoons onion flakes
2 tablespoons grated Parmesan, extra
paprika, to sprinkle

1 Preheat the oven to 180°C (350°F/ Gas 4). Gently squeeze the artichokes to remove any remaining liquid. Chop and place in a bowl. Stir through the mayonnaise, Parmesan and the onion flakes.
2 Spread into a 1-litre capacity shallow ovenproof dish. Sprinkle with the extra Parmesan and a little paprika. Bake for 15 minutes, or until heated through and lightly browned on top. Serve with crusty bread.

NUTRITION PER SERVE
Protein 7 g; Fat 14 g; Carbohydrate 8 g; Dietary Fibre 3 g; Cholesterol 21 mg; 773 kJ (185 cal)

Carefully peel the black and blistered skin away from the baked eggplant.

Process the eggplant, garlic, cumin, lemon, tahini, cayenne and olive oil.

BABA GHANNOUJ

Preparation time: 20 minutes + 30 minutes cooling
Total cooking time: 50 minutes
Serves 10

2 eggplants
3 cloves garlic, crushed
1/2 teaspoon ground cumin
1/3 cup (80 ml/2¾ fl oz) lemon juice
2 tablespoons tahini
pinch cayenne pepper
1½ tablespoons olive oil
1 tablespoon finely chopped fresh flat-leaf
   parsley
black olives, to garnish

1 Preheat the oven to 200°C (400°F/ Gas 6). Pierce the eggplants several times with a fork, then cook over an open flame for about 5 minutes, or until the skin is black and blistering, then place in a roasting tin and bake for 40–45 minutes, or until the eggplants are very soft and wrinkled. Place in a colander over a bowl to drain off any bitter juices and leave to stand for 30 minutes, or until cool.
2 Carefully peel the skin from the eggplant, chop the flesh and place in a food processor with the garlic, cumin, lemon, tahini, cayenne and olive oil. Process until smooth and creamy. Alternatively, use a potato masher or fork. Season with salt and stir in the parsley. Spread onto a flat bowl or plate and garnish with the olives. Serve with flatbread or pide.

NUTRITION PER SERVE
Protein 1.8 g; Fat 5 g; Carbohydrate 3 g; Dietary Fibre 3 g; Cholesterol 0 mg; 269 kJ (64 cal)

NOTE: If you prefer, you can simply roast the eggplant in a roasting tin in a 200°C (400°F/Gas 6) oven for 1 hour, or until very soft and wrinkled. Eggplants are also known as aubergines. The name baba ghannouj can be roughly translated as 'poor man's caviar'.

Mash the blue cheese with a fork to soften it slightly.

Add the cream and yoghurt and season to taste with ground black pepper.

CREAMY BLUE CHEESE DIP WITH PEARS

Preparation time: 25 minutes + 20 minutes refrigeration
Total cooking time: Nil
Serves 4

150 g (5 oz) creamy blue cheese (see NOTE)
200 ml (6½ fl oz) thick cream
3 tablespoons thick plain yoghurt
2 tablespoons finely chopped chives
4 ripe pears, cored and cut into wedges

1 Mash the blue cheese with a fork to soften it slightly. Add the cream and yoghurt and season with black pepper, mixing until smooth and well blended—do not overmix or it will become grainy and curdled. Spoon into a serving bowl, cover and refrigerate for 20 minutes, or until firm.
2 Scatter the chives over the dip. Serve with the pear wedges.

NUTRITION PER SERVE
Protein 10 g; Fat 30 g; Carbohydrate 45 g; Dietary Fibre 8 g; Cholesterol 100 mg; 2042 kJ (488 cal)

NOTE: A creamy cheese such as Dolcelatte, Gorgonzola or King Island Blue will give the best result.

Beat the neufchatel cheese with a wooden spoon until it is smooth.

Add the crab meat, chilli sauce, tomato paste, lemon rind and juice, and onion.

CHILLI CRAB AND TOMATO DIP

Preparation time: 25 minutes
Total cooking time: Nil
Serves 6

2 x 170 g (5½ oz) cans crab meat, drained
200 g (6½ oz) neufchatel cheese (see
   NOTE)
2 tablespoons chilli sauce
2 teaspoons tomato paste
1 teaspoon grated lemon rind
2 teaspoons lemon juice
1 small onion, finely grated
3 spring onions, finely sliced
1 tomato, seeded and finely chopped

1 Squeeze any remaining liquid from the crab meat. Beat the neufchatel cheese until smooth, then add the crab meat, chilli sauce, tomato paste, lemon rind, lemon juice and onion. Season well with salt and pepper. Mix well and spoon into a serving bowl.
2 Scatter the spring onion and chopped tomato over the top and chill before serving.

NUTRITION PER SERVE
Protein 11 g; Fat 11 g; Carbohydrate 6 g; Dietary Fibre 1 g; Cholesterol 79 mg; 682 kJ (163 cal)

NOTE: Neufchatel is a smooth, mild, good-quality cream cheese available from delicatessens.

Quick Dips

Dips are an excellent way to keep friends happy while the barbecue is heating up or cooking larger pieces of meat. These recipes make great use of pantry staples and fridge leftovers, in a truly imaginative manner.

SWEET CHILLI AND SOUR CREAM DIP

Mix 250 g (8 oz) sour cream with 3 tablespoons sweet chilli sauce. Swirl another teaspoon of sweet chilli sauce on top to decorate. Serve with herb and garlic pitta chips, goujons or sweet potato chips. Serves 4

RED PESTO DIP

Mix together 250 g (8 oz) soft cream cheese, 2 tablespoons ready-made red pesto, 1 teaspoon lemon juice and 2 teaspoons chopped fresh flat-leaf parsley. Season with black pepper and serve with herb and garlic pitta chips or savoury biscuits. Serves 4

MUSTARD DIP

Mix together $\frac{1}{2}$ cup (125 g/4 oz) mayonnaise, $\frac{1}{2}$ cup (125 g/4 oz) plain yoghurt, 2 teaspoons Dijon mustard and 3 tablespoons wholegrain mustard. Season well and serve with potato wedges or strips of barbecued chicken. Serves 4

HUMMUS AND ORANGE DIP

Mix together 250 g (8 oz) hummus, 2 tablespoons orange juice, $\frac{1}{4}$ teaspoon ground cumin and 2 teaspoons chopped fresh coriander. Season with pepper and cover with plastic wrap. Refrigerate for 2–3 hours. Serve with sweet potato chips, crisp lavash bread or pitta chips. Serves 4

Top, from left: Mustard Dip; Sweet Chilli and Sour Cream Dip; Creamy Tomato Tuna Dip; Rosemary and Cannellini Bean Dip Bottom, from left: French Onion Dip; Mixed Herb Dip; Red Pesto Dip; Hummus and Orange Dip

ROSEMARY AND CANNELLINI BEAN DIP

Mix a 400 g (13 oz) can rinsed and drained cannellini beans in a food processor with 1 crushed clove garlic, 2 teaspoons chopped fresh rosemary and 1 tablespoon lemon juice for 1 minute. With the motor running, add 2 tablespoons extra virgin olive oil in a thin stream. Season and serve with crisp lavash bread or pitta chips. Serves 4

FRENCH ONION DIP

Use a fork to blend 250 g (8 oz) sour cream with a 30 g (1 oz) packet French onion soup mix. Cover and refrigerate for 1–2 hours. Serve with potato wedges, sweet potato chips or savoury biscuits. Serves 4

CREAMY TOMATO TUNA DIP

Mix 250 g (8 oz) soft cream cheese with a 100 g (3½ oz) can tuna with tomato and onion (including the oil). Add black pepper, cover and refrigerate for 1–2 hours. Serve with sweet chilli chips, lavash bread or potato wedges. Serves 4

MIXED HERB DIP

Chop 15 g (½ oz) chives and mix with 1¼ cups (315 g/ 10 oz) plain yoghurt. Add ¼ cup (7 g/ ¼ oz) fresh marjoram leaves, ¼ cup (5 g/¼ oz) fresh mint leaves and ½ cup (10 g/¼ oz) fresh flat-leaf parsley leaves. Season with black pepper. Serve with lavash bread, pitta or sweet chilli chips. Can also be made with thyme, oregano, garlic chives or dill. Serves 6

Sauces & Salsas

SKORDALIA

Preparation time: 15 minutes
Total cooking time: 10 minutes
Serves 12

500 g (1 lb) floury potatoes (see NOTE)
5 cloves garlic, crushed
ground white pepper
¾ cup (185 ml/6 fl oz) olive oil
2 tablespoons white vinegar

1 Peel the potatoes and cut into small cubes. Cook in boiling water for 10 minutes, or until very soft.
2 Drain the potato and mash until smooth. Stir in the garlic, 1 teaspoon salt and a pinch of white pepper. Gradually pour in the olive oil, mixing well with a wooden spoon. Add the vinegar and season with additional salt and ground white pepper, if needed. Serve as a sauce with barbecued meat, seafood or chicken or as a dip with crusty bread or crackers.

NUTRITION PER SERVE
Protein 1 g; Fat 14.8 g; Carbohydrate 5.6 g; Dietary Fibre 0.9 g; Cholesterol 0 mg; 662 kJ (158 cal)

NOTE: Use King Edward, russet or pontiac potatoes. Do not make skordalia with a food processor—the processing will turn the potato into a gluey mess.

STORAGE: Skordalia will keep in an airtight container for up to 2–3 days in the fridge. The potato will absorb the salt so check the seasoning before serving.

Drain the potato and then mash with a potato masher until smooth.

Gradually add the oil to the potato mixture, mixing with a wooden spoon.

Cut the tomatoes, capsicums, zucchini and eggplants in half lengthways.

Barbecue the vegetables until they are soft and a little blackened.

CHARGRILLED VEGETABLE SALSA

Preparation time: 30 minutes + 2 hours marinating
Total cooking time: 30 minutes
Serves 4

2 Roma tomatoes
1 small red capsicum
1 small green capsicum
2 small zucchini
2 slender eggplants
3 tablespoons olive oil
1 tablespoon chopped fresh flat-leaf parsley
2 teaspoons chopped fresh marjoram
2 teaspoons chopped fresh oregano
2 tablespoons balsamic vinegar
1 tablespoon chopped fresh flat-leaf parsley, extra
2 teaspoons chopped fresh marjoram, extra

1 Halve the tomatoes, capsicums, zucchini and eggplants lengthways. Place in a large shallow dish and pour over the combined olive oil and herbs. Toss well and leave to marinate for at least 2 hours or up to a day.

2 Cook the vegetables on a hot, lightly oiled barbecue flatplate until soft and a little blackened. Place the capsicum in a plastic bag for a few minutes, then peel away the skin. Cut all the vegetables into small pieces and mix with the vinegar and extra herbs. Serve with barbecued meats.

NUTRITION PER SERVE
Protein 3 g; Fat 15 g; Carbohydrate 7 g; Dietary Fibre 5 g; Cholesterol 0 mg; 733 kJ (175 cal)

Mix together the bocconcini, tomato, capsicum and spring onion.

Stir the basil and flat-leaf parsley into the vinaigrette dressing.

BOCCONCINI, TOMATO AND SUN-DRIED CAPSICUM SALSA

Preparation time: 20 minutes
Total cooking time: Nil
Serves 6

180 g (6 oz) bocconcini, diced
200 g (6½ oz) tomatoes, diced
⅓ cup (50 g/1¾ oz) drained sun-dried
   capsicum in oil, chopped
1 spring onion, finely sliced
1 tablespoon extra virgin olive oil
2 teaspoons red wine vinegar
1 tablespoon shredded fresh basil leaves
1 tablespoon chopped fresh flat-leaf parsley

1 Mix together the bocconcini, tomato, sun-dried capsicum and spring onion in a large bowl.
2 Whisk together the oil and vinegar until thoroughly blended. Stir through the basil and parsley.
3 Toss the dressing through the bocconcini and tomato mixture and season well with salt and pepper. Serve at room temperature with barbecued steak or tuna.

NUTRITION PER SERVE
Protein 8 g; Fat 13 g; Carbohydrate 1 g; Dietary Fibre 1 g; Cholesterol 19 mg; 644 kJ (154 cal)

NOTE: Bocconcini are small, fresh mozzarella cheeses.

Place the open rack in the wok or frying pan then put on the onion, capsicum and chilli.

Add the tamarind concentrate to the sauce and simmer, stirring occasionally.

SMOKY TOMATO SAUCE

Preparation time: 15 minutes
Total cooking time: 50 minutes
Makes about 1 litre

SMOKING MIX
2 tablespoons Chinese or Ceylon tea leaves
2 star anise, crushed
1 strip orange rind
1/2 teaspoon five-spice powder
6 juniper berries, crushed

2 onions, quartered
2 red capsicums, cut into large pieces
2 red chillies, cut in half
3 tablespoons oil
3 cloves garlic, chopped
500 g (1 lb) tomatoes, chopped
2 tablespoons Worcestershire sauce
1/2 cup (125 ml/4 fl oz) barbecue sauce

2 tablespoons tamarind concentrate
1 tablespoon white vinegar
1 tablespoon soft brown sugar

1 Combine all the ingredients for the smoking mix in a small bowl. Pour the mix into the centre of a sheet of foil and fold the edges to prevent the mix from spreading. (This will form an open container to allow the mix to smoke.) Place the foil container on the bottom of a dry wok or wide frying pan. Place an open rack or steamer in the wok or frying pan, making sure it is elevated over the mix.
2 Place the onion, capsicum and chilli onto the rack and cover with a lid, or alternatively cover the entire wok or frying pan tightly with foil to prevent the smoke from escaping.
3 Smoke over medium heat for 10–15 minutes, or until the vegetables are tender. If you prefer a very smoky sauce cook the vegetables for longer, if you prefer it less so, reduce the time. Remove the container with the smoking mix.

4 Dice the onion, capsicum and chilli quite finely. Heat the oil in the wok and add the garlic and cooked vegetables. Fry over medium heat for 3 minutes, then add the tomato and cook until pulpy. Add the sauces, tamarind, vinegar and sugar. Simmer, stirring occasionally, for 20–25 minutes, or until the sauce is quite thick. Serve with barbecued meat or seafood. Store in the refrigerator.

NUTRITION PER TABLESPOON
Protein 0.5 g; Fat 1.5 g; Carbohydrate 2.5 g; Dietary Fibre 0.5 g; Cholesterol 0 mg; 90 kJ (20 cal)

NOTE: For a smoother sauce, mix in a food processor for about 30 seconds.

Add the brown sugar to the capsicum mixture and stir over heat until dissolved.

Spoon the thickened relish into the sterilized jars and seal.

RED CAPSICUM RELISH

Preparation time: 40 minutes + a few weeks standing
Total cooking time: 1 hour 45 minutes
Fills three 250 ml (8 fl oz) jars

1 kg (2 lb) red capsicums
1 teaspoon black peppercorns
2 teaspoons black mustard seeds
2 red onions, thinly sliced
4 cloves garlic, chopped
1½ cups (375 ml/12 fl oz) red wine vinegar
2 apples, peeled, cored and grated
1 teaspoon grated fresh ginger
1 cup (230 g/7½ oz) soft brown sugar

1 Remove the capsicum seeds and membrane and thinly slice. Tie the peppercorns in a piece of muslin and secure with string. Combine the capsicum, peppercorns, mustard seeds, onion, garlic, vinegar, apple and ginger in a large pan. Simmer for 30 minutes until the capsicum is soft.
2 Add the sugar and stir over low heat until completely dissolved. Simmer, stirring occasionally, for 1¼ hours, or until the relish has reduced and thickened. Remove the muslin bag.
3 Rinse the jars with boiling water then dry in a warm oven. Spoon the relish into the hot jars and seal. Turn the jars upside down for 2 minutes, then turn them the other way up and leave to cool. Label and date. Leave for a few weeks before using. Will keep in a cool dark place for 1 year. Refrigerate after opening.

NUTRITION PER TABLESPOON
Protein 0.5 g; Fat 0 g; Carbohydrate 85 g; Dietary Fibre 0.5 g; Cholesterol 0 mg; 160 kJ (40 cal)

Cook the onion and garlic over low heat, then add the chilli and shrimp paste.

Bring to the boil, stirring, then add the kecap manis and tomato sauce.

SATAY SAUCE

Preparation time: 10 minutes
Total cooking time: 15 minutes
Serves 8

1 tablespoon oil
1 large onion, finely chopped
2 cloves garlic, finely chopped
2 red chillies, finely chopped
1 teaspoon shrimp paste
1 cup (250 g/8 oz) peanut butter
1 cup (250 ml/8 fl oz) coconut milk
2 teaspoons kecap manis or thick soy sauce
1 tablespoon tomato sauce

1 Heat the oil in a pan and cook the onion and garlic for 8 minutes over low heat, stirring regularly. Add the chilli and shrimp paste, cook for 1 minute and remove from the heat.
2 Add the peanut butter, return to the heat and stir in the coconut milk and 1 cup (250 ml/8 fl oz) water. Bring to the boil over low heat, stirring so that it does not stick. Add the kecap manis and tomato sauce and simmer for 1 minute. Cool and serve with skewered meats or seafood.

NUTRITION PER SERVE

Protein 9 g; Fat 25 g; Carbohydrate 6 g; Dietary Fibre 4 g; Cholesterol 0 mg; 1148 kJ (274 cal)

Cook the onion over low heat, stirring occasionally, until soft.

Add the remaining ingredients to the pan and bring to the boil.

BARBECUE SAUCE

Preparation time: 15 minutes
Total cooking time: 10 minutes
Serves 4

2 teaspoons oil
1 small onion, finely chopped
1 tablespoon malt vinegar
1 tablespoon soft brown sugar
1/3 cup (80 ml/2¾ fl oz) tomato sauce
1 tablespoon Worcestershire sauce

1 Heat the oil in a small pan and cook the onion over low heat for 3 minutes, or until soft, stirring occasionally.
2 Add the remaining ingredients and bring to the boil. Reduce the heat and simmer for 3 minutes, stirring occasionally. Serve warm or at room temperature. Can be kept, covered and refrigerated, for up to a week. Serve with burgers or barbecued meat.

NUTRITION PER SERVE
Protein 1 g; Fat 1 g; Carbohydrate 17 g; Dietary Fibre 1 g; Cholesterol 0 mg; 648 kJ (155 cal)

Desserts

PEACHES POACHED IN WINE

Preparation time: 20 minutes
Total cooking time: 20 minutes
Serves 4

4 just-ripe yellow-fleshed slipstone peaches
   (see NOTE)
2 cups (500 ml/16 fl oz) sweet white wine
   such as Sauternes
3 tablespoons orange liqueur
1 cup (250 g/8 oz) sugar
1 cinnamon stick
1 vanilla bean, split
8 fresh mint leaves
mascarpone or crème fraîche, to serve

1 Cut a small cross in the base of each peach.
Immerse the peaches in boiling water for 30
seconds, then drain and cool slightly. Peel off
the skin, cut in half and carefully remove the
stones.
2 Place the wine, liqueur, sugar, cinnamon
stick and vanilla bean in a deep-sided frying pan
large enough to hold the peach halves in a
single layer. Heat the mixture, stirring, until the
sugar dissolves. Bring to the boil, then reduce
the heat and simmer for 5 minutes. Add the
peaches to the pan and simmer for 4 minutes,
turning them over halfway through. Remove with
a slotted spoon and leave to cool. Continue to
simmer the syrup for 6–8 minutes, or until
thick. Strain and set aside.
3 Arrange the peaches on a serving platter, cut-
side-up. Spoon the syrup over the top and
garnish each half with a mint leaf. Serve the
peaches warm or chilled, with a dollop of
mascarpone or crème fraîche.

NUTRITION PER SERVE
Protein 3 g; Fat 6.5 g; Carbohydrate 74 g;
Dietary Fibre 2 g; Cholesterol 19 mg; 1900 kJ
(455 cal)

NOTE: There are two types of peach, the
slipstone and the clingstone. As the names
imply, clingstone indicates that the flesh will
cling to the stone whereas the stones in
slipstone or freestone peaches are easily
removed without breaking up the flesh. Each has
a variety with either yellow or white flesh, and
all these peaches are equally delicious.

Peel the skin away from the cross cut in the base of
the peaches.

Simmer the wine, liqueur, sugar, cinnamon and
vanilla bean.

Using a slotted spoon, remove the figs from the pan of syrup.

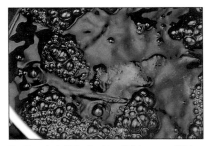

Continue to boil the liquid until it becomes thick and syrupy.

FIGS IN HONEY SYRUP

Preparation time: 15 minutes
Total cooking time: 1 hour
Serves 4

100 g (3½ oz) blanched whole almonds
12–16 whole fresh figs (see NOTE)
½ cup (125 g/4 oz) sugar
⅓ cup (115 g/4 oz) honey
2 tablespoons lemon juice
5 cm (2 inch) sliver of lemon rind
1 cinnamon stick
1 cup (250 g/8 oz) Greek-style plain yoghurt

1 Preheat the oven to 180°C (350°F/ Gas 4). Place the almonds on a baking tray and bake for 5 minutes, or until golden brown. Cool. Cut the tops off the figs and make a small incision down the top of each one. Push an almond into the base of each fig. Roughly chop the remaining almonds.
2 Place 3 cups (750 ml/24 fl oz) water in a large saucepan, add the sugar and stir over medium heat until the sugar dissolves. Increase the heat and bring to the boil. Stir in the honey, juice, rind and cinnamon stick. Reduce the heat, add the figs and cook for 30 minutes. Remove with a slotted spoon.
3 Boil the liquid over high heat for 15–20 minutes, or until thick and syrupy. Remove the cinnamon and rind. Cool the syrup slightly and pour over the figs. Sprinkle with the remaining almonds. Serve warm or cold with yoghurt.

NUTRITION PER SERVE
Protein 11 g; Fat 17 g; Carbohydrate 74 g; Dietary Fibre 7 g; Cholesterol 10 mg; 2017 kJ (482 cal)

NOTE: You can also use 500 g dried whole figs. Cover with 3 cups (750 ml) cold water and soak for 8 hours. Drain, reserving the liquid. Push a blanched almond into the bottom of each fig. Place the liquid in a large saucepan, add the sugar and bring to the boil, stirring as the sugar dissolves. Add the honey, lemon juice, lemon rind and cinnamon stick, and continue the recipe as above.

Scrape the frozen edges of the mixture back into the centre.

Beat the granita mixture with a fork just prior to serving to break up the crystals.

LEMON GRANITA

Preparation time: 15 minutes + 2 hours freezing
Total cooking time: 5 minutes
Serves 6

1¼ cups (315 ml/10 fl oz) lemon juice
1 tablespoon lemon zest
200 g (61/2 oz) caster sugar

1 Place the lemon juice, lemon zest and caster sugar in a small saucepan and stir over low heat for 5 minutes, or until the sugar is dissolved. Remove from the heat and leave to cool.
2 Add 2 cups (500 ml/16 fl oz) water to the juice mixture and mix together well. Pour the mixture into a shallow 30 x 20 cm (12 x 8 inch) metal container and place in the freezer until the mixture is beginning to freeze around the edges. Scrape the frozen sections back into the mixture with a fork. Repeat every 30 minutes until the mixture has even-size ice crystals. Beat the mixture with a fork just before serving. To serve, spoon the lemon granita into six chilled glasses.

NUTRITION PER SERVE
Protein 0 g; Fat 0 g; Carbohydrate 35 g; Dietary Fibre 0 g; Cholesterol 0 mg; 592 kJ (140 cal)

Boil the sugar, wine, star anise, lemon rind and water for 3 minutes.

Mix together the strawberries, blueberries, raspberries, cherries and plums.

RED FRUIT SALAD WITH BERRIES

Preparation time: 5 minutes + 30 minutes cooling + 1 hour 30 minutes refrigeration
Total cooking time: 5 minutes
Serves 6

SYRUP
1/4 cup (60 g/2 oz) caster sugar
1/2 cup (125 ml/4 fl oz) dry red wine
1 star anise
1 teaspoon finely chopped lemon rind

250 g (8 oz) strawberries, hulled and halved
150 g (5 oz) blueberries
150 g (5 oz) raspberries, mulberries or other red berries

250 g (8 oz) cherries
5 small red plums (about 250 g (8 oz)), stones removed and quartered
low-fat yoghurt, to serve

1 To make the syrup, place the sugar, wine, star anise, lemon rind and 1/2 cup (125 ml/4 fl oz) water in a small saucepan. Bring to the boil over medium heat, stirring to dissolve the sugar. Boil the syrup for 3 minutes, then set aside to cool for 30 minutes. When cool, strain the syrup.
2 Mix the fruit together in a large bowl and pour on the red wine syrup. Mix well to coat the fruit in the syrup and refrigerate for 1 hour 30 minutes. Serve the fruit dressed with a little syrup and the yoghurt.

NUTRITION PER SERVE
Fat 0 g; Protein 2 g; Carbohydrate 24 g; Dietary Fibre 5 g; Cholesterol 0 mg; 500 kJ (120 Cal)

Sprinkle the caster sugar evenly over the strawberries and toss to coat.

Use good-quality balsamic vinegar to sprinkle over the strawberries.

STRAWBERRIES WITH BALSAMIC VINEGAR

Preparation time: 10 minutes + 2 hours 30 minutes marinating
Total cooking time: Nil
Serves 4

750 g (1½ lb) small ripe strawberries
¼ cup (60 g/2 oz) caster sugar
2 tablespoons balsamic vinegar
½ cup (125 g/4 oz) mascarpone

1 Wipe the strawberries with a clean damp cloth and carefully remove the green stalks. If the strawberries are large, cut each one in half.
2 Place all the strawberries in a large glass bowl, sprinkle the caster sugar evenly over the top and toss gently to coat. Set aside for 2 hours to macerate, then sprinkle the balsamic vinegar over the strawberries. Toss them again, then refrigerate for about 30 minutes.
3 Spoon the strawberries into four glasses, drizzle with the syrup and top with a dollop of mascarpone.

NUTRITION PER SERVE
Protein 6 g; Fat 11 g; Carbohydrate 20 g; Dietary Fibre 4 g; Cholesterol 30 mg; 830 kJ (200 cal)

NOTE: If you leave the strawberries for more than 2 hours, it is best to refrigerate them.

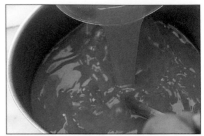

Stir the mandarin juice into the saucepan of sugar water.

Blend the frozen mixture in a food processor until it is slushy.

MANDARIN ICE

Preparation time: 10 minutes + freezing
Total cooking time: 10 minutes
Serves 4–6

10 mandarins
$^1/_2$ cup (125 g/4 oz) caster sugar

1 Squeeze the mandarins to make 2 cups (500 ml/16 fl oz) juice.
2 Place the sugar and 1 cup (250 ml/ 8 fl oz) water in a small saucepan. Stir over low heat until the sugar has dissolved, then simmer for 5 minutes. Remove from the heat and leave to cool slightly.
3 Stir the mandarin juice into the sugar syrup, then pour into a shallow metal tray. Freeze for 2 hours, or until frozen. Transfer to a food processor and blend until slushy. Return to the freezer and repeat the process three more times.

NUTRITION PER SERVE (6)
Fat 0 g; Protein 0.5 g; Carbohydrate 5 g; Dietary Fibre 0 g; Cholesterol 0 mg; 105 kJ (25 Cal)

Leave the jelly to cool completely before removing the lemon and orange rind.

Put the berries in the wine glasses and then pour jelly over the top.

BERRIES IN CHAMPAGNE JELLY

Preparation time: 10 minutes + overnight refrigeration
Total cooking time: 5 minutes
Serves 8

1 litre Champagne or sparkling white wine
1½ tablespoons gelatine
1 cup (250 g/8 oz) sugar
4 strips lemon rind
4 strips orange rind
250 g (8 oz) small hulled and halved strawberries
250 g (8 oz) blueberries

1 Pour 2 cups (500 ml) Champagne into a bowl and let the bubbles subside. Sprinkle the gelatine over the Champagne in an even layer. Leave until the gelatine is spongy—do not stir. Place the remaining Champagne in a large saucepan with the sugar, lemon and orange rind, and heat gently, stirring, for 3–4 minutes until all the sugar has dissolved.

2 Remove the pan from the heat, add the gelatine mixture and stir until thoroughly dissolved. Leave the jelly to cool completely, then remove the lemon and orange rind.

3 Divide the berries among eight ½ cup (125 ml/ 4 fl oz) wine glasses and gently pour the jelly over the top. Refrigerate for 6 hours or overnight, or until fully set. Remove from the fridge 15 minutes before serving.

NUTRITION PER SERVE
Protein 3 g; Fat 0 g; Carbohydrate 37 g; Dietary Fibre 1 g; Cholesterol 0 mg; 965 kJ (230 cal)

Add the eggs one at a time to the cream cheese mixture and beat well.

When the filling is smooth, mix in the vanilla, orange juice and rind.

BAKED CHEESECAKE

Preparation time: 30 minutes + 20 minutes refrigeration + chilling
Total cooking time: 55 minutes
Serves 8

250 g (8 oz) butternut cookies
1 teaspoon mixed spice
100 g (3¹/₂ oz) butter, melted
500 g (1 lb) cream cheese, softened
²/₃ cup (160 g/5¹/₂ oz) caster sugar
4 eggs
1 teaspoon vanilla essence
1 tablespoon orange juice
1 tablespoon finely grated orange rind

TOPPING
1 cup (250 g/8 oz) sour cream
¹/₂ teaspoon vanilla essence
3 teaspoons orange juice
1 tablespoon caster sugar
freshly grated nutmeg

1 Lightly grease the base of a 20 cm (8 inch) springform tin. Finely crush the biscuits in a food processor for 30 seconds, or put them in a plastic bag and roll with a rolling pin. Transfer to a bowl and add the mixed spice and butter. Stir until all the crumbs are moistened, then spoon into the tin and press firmly into the base and side. Chill for 20 minutes, or until firm.

2 Preheat the oven to 180°C (350°F/ Gas 4). Beat the cream cheese until smooth. Add the sugar and beat until smooth. Add the eggs, one at a time, beating well after each addition. Mix in the vanilla, orange juice and rind.

3 Pour the mixture into the crumb case and bake for 45 minutes, or until just firm. To make the topping, combine the sour cream, vanilla, orange juice and sugar in a bowl. Spread over the hot cheesecake, sprinkle with nutmeg and return to the oven for 7 minutes. Cool, then refrigerate until firm.

NUTRITION PER SERVE

Protein 10 g; Fat 50 g; Carbohydrate 45 g; Dietary Fibre 0.5 g; Cholesterol 230 mg; 2885 kJ (690 cal)

Fold the beaten egg whites gently into the cream mixture with a metal spoon.

Dip half the biscuits in the coffee mixture, drain, and arrange in the serving dish.

TIRAMISU

Preparation time: 30 minutes + 2 hours refrigeration
Total cooking time: Nil
Serves 6

3 cups (750 ml/24 fl oz) strong black coffee, cooled
3 tablespoons Marsala or coffee-flavored liqueur
2 eggs, separated
3 tablespoons caster sugar
250 g (8 oz) mascarpone
1 cup (250 ml/8 fl oz) cream, whipped
16 large sponge fingers
2 tablespoons dark cocoa powder

1 Mix together the coffee and Marsala in a bowl and set aside. Using electric beaters, beat the egg yolks and sugar in a bowl for 3 minutes, or until thick and pale. Add the mascarpone and mix until just combined. Transfer to a large bowl and fold in the cream.

2 Beat the egg whites until soft peaks form. Fold quickly and lightly into the cream mixture.

3 Dip half the biscuits into the coffee mixture, then drain off any excess coffee and arrange in the base of a 2.5 litre ceramic dish. Spread half the cream mixture over the biscuits.

4 Dip the remaining biscuits into the remaining coffee mixture and repeat the layers. Smooth the surface and dust liberally with the cocoa powder. Refrigerate for at least 2 hours, or until firm.

NUTRITION PER SERVE
Protein 7.5 g; Fat 24 g; Carbohydrate 28 g; Dietary Fibre 1 g; Cholesterol 180 mg; 1545 kJ (370 cal)

STORAGE: Tiramisu is best made a day in advance to let the flavors develop. Refrigerate until ready to serve.

Check if the fruit is tender by poking with the tip of a sharp knife.

Blend the partially frozen mixture in a food processor until smooth.

APPLE AND PEAR SORBET

Preparation time: 10 minutes + freezing
Total cooking time: 10 minutes
Serves 4–6

4 large green apples, peeled, cored and chopped
4 pears, peeled, cored and chopped
1 strip of lemon rind
1 cinnamon stick
¼ cup (60 m/2 fl ozl) lemon juice
4 tablespoons caster sugar
2 tablespoons Calvados or poire William liqueur (optional)

1 Place the apple and pear in a large deep saucepan with the lemon rind, cinnamon stick and enough water to just cover the fruit. Cover and poach the fruit gently over medium–low heat for 6–8 minutes, or until tender. Remove the lemon rind and cinnamon stick. Place the fruit in a food processor and blend with the lemon juice until smooth.
2 Place the sugar in a saucepan with 80 ml (2¾ fl oz) water, bring to the boil and simmer for 1 minute. Add the fruit purée and the liqueur and combine well.
3 Pour into a shallow metal tray and freeze for 2 hours, or until the mixture is frozen around the edges. Transfer to a food processor or bowl and blend or beat until smooth. Pour back into the tray and return to the freezer. Repeat this process three times. For the final freezing, place in an airtight container—cover the surface with a piece of greaseproof paper and cover with a lid. Serve in small glasses or bowls.

NUTRITION PER SERVE (6)
Fat 0.5 g; Protein 1 g; Carbohydrate 42 g; Dietary Fibre 4.5 g; Cholesterol 0 mg; 730 kJ (175 Cal)

HINT: Pour an extra nip of Calvados over the sorbet to serve.

Spoon half the jelly over the biscuits before scattering on half the strawberries.

Dip the remaining biscuits in the brandy mixture and layer evenly over the custard.

STRAWBERRY TRIFLE

Preparation time: 20 minutes + 4 hours refrigeration
Total cooking time: Nil
Serves 8

2 x 85 g (3 oz) packets red jelly crystals
1 cup (250 ml/8 fl oz) brandy or rum
1 cup (250 ml/8 fl oz) milk
2 x 250 g (8 oz) packets thin sponge finger biscuits
500 g (1 lb) strawberries, sliced
750 ml (24 fl oz) carton custard
1¼ cups (315 ml/10 fl oz) cream, whipped

1 Mix the jelly crystals with 1¾ cups (440 ml/ 14 fl oz) of boiling water and stir to dissolve. Pour into a shallow tin and refrigerate until the jelly has just set but is not firm.

2 Combine the brandy and milk in a dish. Dip half the biscuits in the brandy mixture then place in a single layer in a 3-litre glass or ceramic dish. Spoon half the jelly over the biscuits. Scatter with half the strawberries and then half of the custard.

3 Dip the remaining sponge fingers in the brandy mixture and place evenly over the custard, followed by the remaining jelly and custard. Spread the whipped cream evenly over the custard and top with the remaining strawberries. Cover and refrigerate for 4 hours before serving.

NUTRITION PER SERVE
Protein 13 g; Fat 24 g; Carbohydrate 75 g; Dietary Fibre 2 g; Cholesterol 165 mg; 2570 kJ (615 cal)

Mix the gelatine with the water and then stir into the lime curd.

To make the glazed lime rind, simmer the lime for 3 minutes in sugar syrup, then drain on a rack.

CREAMY LIME TART

Preparation time: 30 minutes + 20 minutes refrigeration
Total cooking time: 1 hour
Serves 12

1¼ cups (155 g/5 oz) plain flour
½ cup (95 g/3 oz) ground almonds
90 g (3 oz) butter, chopped

FILLING
6 egg yolks
½ cup (125 g/4 oz) caster sugar
100 g (3½ oz) butter, melted
⅓ cup (80 ml/2¾ fl oz) lime juice
2 teaspoons finely grated lime rind
2 teaspoons gelatine
½ cup (125 ml/4 fl oz) cream, whipped
½ cup (125 g/4 oz) sugar
rind of 4 limes, finely shredded

1 Preheat the oven to 180°C (350°F/ Gas 4). Sift the flour into a large bowl and add the almonds and butter. Rub in the butter until fine and crumbly. Add 1–2 tablespoons cold water and mix to a firm dough, adding more if necessary. Turn out onto a lightly floured surface and roll out to fit a 23 cm (9 inch) fluted flan tin. Trim the edge and refrigerate for 20 minutes.
2 Line with baking paper and beads or dried beans or rice and bake for 20 minutes. Remove the paper and beads and bake the pastry shell for a further 20 minutes, or until lightly golden. Cool completely.
3 To make the filling, put the egg yolks, sugar, butter, lime juice and rind in a heatproof bowl. Whisk together to dissolve the sugar. Place the bowl over a pan of simmering water and stir constantly for 15 minutes, or until thickened. Leave to cool slightly.
4 Put the gelatine and 1 tablespoon water in a small bowl. Leave until spongy, then stir until dissolved. Stir into the lime curd. Cool to room temperature, stirring occasionally.

5 Fold the cream through the lime curd and pour into the pastry case. Refrigerate for 2–3 hours until set, removing 15 minutes before serving. Put the sugar in a small pan with 3 tablespoons water. Stir without boiling until the sugar has completely dissolved. Bring to the boil, add the lime rind and simmer for 3 minutes. Remove the rind and dry on a rack then use to decorate the tart.

NUTRITION PER SERVE
Protein 4 g; Fat 21 g; Carbohydrate 32 g; Dietary Fibre 1 g; Cholesterol 144 mg; 1391 kJ (332 cal)

Stir the gelatine sheets into the hot liquid until they have dissolved.

Divide the lychees among the wine glasses, gently dropping them into the jelly.

GINGER AND LYCHEE JELLY

Preparation time: 10 minutes + 4 hours setting
Total cooking time: 5 minutes
Serves 6

500 g (1 lb) can lychees
2 cups (500 ml/16 fl oz) clear apple juice (no added sugar)
1/3 cup (80 ml/2¾ fl oz) strained lime juice
2 tablespoons caster sugar
3 x 3 cm (1 x 1 inch) piece fresh ginger, peeled and thinly sliced
4 sheets gelatine
fresh mint, to garnish

1 Drain the syrup from the lychees and reserve 1 cup (250 ml/8 fl oz) of the syrup. Place the reserved syrup, apple juice, lime juice, sugar and ginger in a saucepan. Bring to the boil, then simmer for 5 minutes. Strain into a heatproof bowl.

2 Place the gelatine sheets in a large bowl of cold water and soak for 2 minutes, or until they soften. Squeeze out the excess water, then add to the syrup. Stir until dissolved. Leave to cool.

3 Pour 2 tablespoons of jelly into each of six 150 ml (5 fl oz) wine glasses, and divide the lychees among the wine glasses. Refrigerate until the jelly has set. Spoon the remaining jelly over the fruit and refrigerate until set. Garnish with mint leaves.

NUTRITION PER SERVE
Fat 0 g; Protein 1 g; Carbohydrate 31 g; Dietary Fibre 0.5 g; Cholesterol 0 mg; 530 kJ (125 Cal)

Spread the meringue onto the paper-lined tray, using the circle as a guide.

Just before serving, spread the cooled meringue with the whipped cream.

PAVLOVA

Preparation time: 15 minutes
Total cooking time: 40 minutes
Serves 8

6 egg whites
1½ cups (375 g/12 oz) caster sugar
1 cup (250 ml/8 fl oz) cream, whipped
125 g (4 oz) strawberries, halved
2 kiwi fruit, peeled and sliced
1 banana, sliced
pulp of 2 passionfruit

1 Preheat the oven to 150°C (300°F/ Gas 2). Line a tray with baking paper and mark with a 22 cm (9 inch) circle. Beat the egg whites until soft peaks form. Gradually beat in the sugar, then beat for several minutes, or until thick and glossy.
2 Spoon the meringue mixture onto the circle on the tray. Smooth the edge and top with a flat-bladed knife.
3 Bake for 40 minutes, or until pale and crisp. Turn off the oven and leave the meringue inside to cool, with the door propped ajar. Just before serving, spread with cream and top with strawberries, kiwi fruit, banana and passionfruit pulp.

NUTRITION PER SERVE
Protein 3 g; Fat 14 g; Carbohydrate 52 g; Dietary Fibre 1 g; Cholesterol 40 mg; 901 kJ (215 cal)

STORAGE: Pavlova can be made 1 day in advance and stored in an airtight container. Top with cream and fruit just before serving.

Mix together the honey, butter, cardamom, rum and sugar to make the syrup.

Cook the kebabs on a hot barbecue, brushing with the syrup during cooking.

FRUIT KEBABS WITH CARDAMOM SYRUP

Preparation time: 15 minutes + 1 hour marinating
Total cooking time: 5 minutes
Makes 8 kebabs

¹/₄ small pineapple, peeled
1 peach
1 banana, peeled
16 strawberries

CARDAMOM SYRUP
2 tablespoons honey
30 g (1 oz) butter, melted
¹/₂ teaspoon ground cardamom
1 tablespoon rum or brandy
1 tablespoon soft brown sugar

1 Cut the pineapple into bite-sized pieces. Cut the peach into 8 wedges and slice the banana. Thread all the fruit pieces onto skewers and place in a shallow dish.
2 To make the cardamom syrup, mix together the honey, butter, cardamom, rum and sugar and pour over the kebabs, brushing to coat. Cover and leave the kebabs at room temperature for 1 hour.
3 Cook the kebabs on a hot, lightly oiled barbecue flatplate for 5 minutes. Brush with the syrup during cooking. Serve drizzled with the remaining syrup, topped with ice cream.

NUTRITION PER KEBAB
Protein 1 g; Fat 2 g; Carbohydrate 16 g; Dietary Fibre 2 g; Cholesterol 6 mg; 376 kJ (90 cal)

Beat the cream cheese and sugar together and then add the lemon juice.

Arrange layers of pear slices and then the cream cheese filling.

GINGER PEAR CHEESECAKE

Preparation time: 25 minutes + 3 hours refrigeration
Total cooking time: Nil
Serves 8

250 g (8 oz) gingersnap biscuits
2 tablespoons caster sugar
125 g (4 oz) butter, melted

FILLING
1 tablespoon gelatine
375 g (12 oz) cream cheese
1/3 cup (90 g/3 oz) caster sugar
1 tablespoon lemon juice
1 cup (250 ml/8 fl oz) cream, whipped
425 g (14 oz) can pear halves, drained and sliced
2 tablespoons chopped glacé ginger

1 Brush a 20 cm (8 inch) springform tin with melted butter or oil. Chop the biscuits to crumbs in a food processor. Transfer to a bowl, add the sugar and butter and mix well. Press firmly into the tin and refrigerate for 20 minutes.
2 To make the filling, put the gelatine in a small bowl with 3 tablespoons water. Leave until spongy, then stir until dissolved. Beat the cream cheese until softened. Add the caster sugar and beat for 3 minutes. Add the lemon juice and beat until combined. Add a little of this mixture to the gelatine and mix well, then add all the gelatine to the filling mixture. Fold in the whipped cream.
3 Arrange a layer of pear slices on the biscuit crust, then pour over half the filling. Top with another layer of pears and the remaining filling. Refrigerate for 3 hours or until set. Decorate with chopped glacé ginger.

NUTRITION PER SERVE
Protein 6 g; Fat 42 g; Carbohydrate 43 g; Dietary Fibre 1 g; Cholesterol 128 mg; 2372 kJ (567 cal)

Add the egg yolks to the cooled chocolate and cream mixture.

Just before you are ready to serve, spread the topping over the flan.

CHOCOLATE MOUSSE FLAN

Preparation time: 35 minutes
Total cooking time: 5 minutes
Serves 10

250 g (8 oz) plain chocolate biscuits, finely crushed
125 g (4 oz) butter, melted

FILLING
200 g (6½ oz) dark cooking chocolate, chopped
2 tablespoons cream
2 egg yolks
2 teaspoons gelatine
²/₃ cup cream (170 ml/5½ fl oz), extra, whipped
2 egg whites

TOPPING
1½ teaspoons instant coffee
1 cup (250 ml/8 fl oz) cream
1 tablespoon caster sugar
cocoa powder, for dusting

1 Brush a 28 cm (11 inch) round fluted flan tin with melted butter or oil. Line the base with paper. Mix the biscuit crumbs and butter and press into the tin. Refrigerate until firm.
2 To make the filling, put the chocolate and cream in a small pan. Stir over low heat until smooth. Cool slightly, then stir in the yolks. Sprinkle the gelatine over 1 tablespoon water in a small bowl and leave until spongy, then stir. Cool slightly and stir into the filling. Fold in the whipped cream.
3 Beat the egg whites until soft peaks form. Fold into the filling and spread over the biscuit base. Refrigerate until set. Just before serving, remove from the tin and spread with the topping.

4 To make the topping, dissolve the coffee in 3 teaspoons water. Stir in the cream and sugar. Beat until soft peaks form, then spread over the flan. Dust with sifted cocoa powder to serve.

NUTRITION PER SERVE
Protein 6 g; Fat 37 g; Carbohydrate 32 g; Dietary Fibre 1 g; Cholesterol 158 mg; 1983 kJ (474 cal)

Mix together the desiccated coconut, lime rind, lime juice and coconut milk powder.

Add the coconut mixture to the ice cream and fold in with a large metal spoon.

COCONUT LIME ICE CREAM

Preparation time: 10 minutes + 30 minutes freezing
Total cooking time: Nil
Serves 4

¼ cup (30 g/1 oz) desiccated coconut
1½ tablespoons grated lime rind
⅓ cup (80 ml/2¾ fl oz) lime juice
4 tablespoons coconut milk powder
1 litre good-quality vanilla ice cream, softened
coconut macaroon biscuits, to serve

1 Put the coconut, lime rind, lime juice and coconut milk powder in a bowl and mix together well.
2 Add to the ice cream and fold through with a large metal spoon until evenly incorporated. Work quickly so that the ice cream does not melt. Return the ice cream to the freezer and freeze for 30 minutes to firm. Serve in glasses with coconut macaroons.

NUTRITION PER SERVE
Protein 5 g; Fat 19.5 g; Carbohydrate 19 g; Dietary Fibre 1.5 g; Cholesterol 30 mg; 1230 kJ (293 cal)

Use a vegetable peeler to remove 3 strips of the orange rind.

Put the apple juice, whole spices and thick strips of rind in a pan with water.

POACHED DRIED FRUIT WITH WHOLE SPICES

Preparation time: 10 minutes + 2 hours soaking
Total cooking time: 30 minutes
Serves 8

1 orange
1 lemon
1 cup (250 ml/8 fl oz) apple juice
6 whole cardamom pods, lightly crushed
6 whole cloves
1 cinnamon stick
1/2 vanilla bean
375 g (12 oz) packet dried fruit salad
1/2 cup (125 g/4 oz) sugar
3 tablespoons soft brown sugar
1 tablespoon brandy

1 Peel 3 large strips of orange rind, avoiding too much white pith. Peel the lemon rind into thick strips. Cut half the rind into thin strips.
2 Put the apple juice, whole spices and thick strips of rind in a large pan with 3 cups (750 ml/ 24 fl oz) water and bring to the boil. Add the dried fruit. Remove from the heat and set aside for 2 hours.
3 Return to the heat, add the combined sugars and thin strips of rind and cover. Cook over low heat for 5 minutes, or until soft. Remove the fruit with a slotted spoon. Simmer the juice for another 5 minutes, or until reduced and thickened slightly. Add the brandy. Serve the fruit warm or cold, drizzled with juice.

NUTRITION PER SERVE
Protein 1 g; Fat 0.5 g; Carbohydrate 58 g; Dietary Fibre 3 g; Cholesterol 0 mg; 994 kJ (237 cal)

STORAGE: This will keep well for at least a week.

Beat the butter and sugar, then add the vanilla essence and egg.

Brush the top of the slice with milk and then sprinkle with sugar and cinnamon.

SPICED APPLE SLICE

Preparation time: 25 minutes + 30 minutes refrigeration
Total cooking time: 55 minutes
Serves 8

750 g (1½ lb) green apples
⅓ cup (90 g/3 oz) sugar
½ teaspoon ground cloves
2 tablespoons lemon juice
1 cup (125 g/4 oz) plain flour
1 cup (125 g/4 oz) self-raising flour
1 teaspoon ground cloves, extra
½ teaspoon ground cinnamon
150 g (5 oz) butter
½ cup (125 g/4 oz) caster sugar
1 teaspoon vanilla essence
1 egg, lightly beaten
1 tablespoon milk
1 tablespoon caster sugar, extra
1 teaspoon ground cinnamon, extra

1 Brush a 20 x 30 cm (8 x 12 inch) shallow tin with oil. Line the base with paper and grease the paper. Preheat the oven to 180°C (350°F/Gas 4). Peel, core and slice the apples and put in a pan with the sugar, cloves and juice. Stir over heat to warm. Cover and simmer, stirring often, for 20 minutes or until soft. Remove from the heat, drain and cool.

2 Sift the flours with the extra cloves and cinnamon. Beat the butter and sugar until light and creamy. Add the vanilla and egg and beat thoroughly. Fold in the flour in batches, mixing after each addition. If the mixture is too dry, add a little milk. Knead gently on a lightly floured surface until smooth. Divide in half, cover with plastic wrap and chill for 30 minutes.

3 Roll out one portion of pastry to fit the tin base. Spread with apple filling. Place the second pastry sheet on top of the filling and press down gently.

4 Brush the top with milk and sprinkle with the extra sugar and cinnamon. Bake for 30 minutes or until golden brown. Leave for 15 minutes, then turn onto a wire rack to cool.

NUTRITION PER SERVE

Protein 5 g; Fat 17 g; Carbohydrate 64 g; Dietary Fibre 3 g; Cholesterol 72 mg; 1772 kJ (423 cal)

Add the warm chocolate mixture slowly, through a strainer, discarding the mint.

If you don't have an ice-cream machine, freeze the mixture and then beat.

CHOCOLATE MINT ICE CREAM

Preparation time: 25 minutes + freezing
Total cooking time: 10 minutes
Serves 6

1 cup (250 ml/8 fl oz) cream
3 tablespoons chopped fresh mint
100 g (3½ oz) dark chocolate, broken
60 g (2 oz) milk chocolate, broken
2 eggs, lightly beaten
1 tablespoon caster sugar

1 Place the cream and mint in a small pan. Stir over low heat until the cream is almost boiling. Cool slightly. Add the chocolate to the cream. Stir over low heat until the chocolate has melted and the mixture is smooth.

2 Whisk the eggs and sugar in a small bowl until creamy. Gradually add the warm chocolate mixture through a strainer. Discard the mint. Whisk until well combined and then cool.

3 Freeze the mixture in an ice-cream machine according to the manufacturer's instructions. Alternatively, freeze in a metal container until just firm around the edges. Remove from the freezer and beat for 1 minute. Return to the freezer and freeze overnight.

NUTRITION PER SERVE
Protein 5 g; Fat 27 g; Carbohydrate 21 g; Dietary Fibre 0 g; Cholesterol 118 mg; 1413 kJ (338 cal)

STORAGE: Ice cream can be stored in the freezer for up to 3 weeks.

Bring the lemon juice, sugar, cloves, mint and water to the boil and add the apple.

Put the apple in a bowl and then pour the syrup over the top through a sieve.

POACHED APPLES WITH CLOVES, MINT AND BASIL

Preparation time: 15 minutes
Total cooking time: 30 minutes
Serves 4

4 large or 6 small green apples
2 tablespoons lemon juice
$1/2$ cup (125 g/4 oz) sugar
4 whole cloves
4 fresh mint sprigs
6 fresh basil leaves

1 Peel and core the apples and cut into quarters. Put the lemon juice, sugar, cloves and mint in a pan with 625 ml (21 fl oz) water. Stir over low heat without boiling until the sugar dissolves. Bring to the boil.
2 Add the apple to the pan. Cook over low heat, partially covered, for 10 minutes or until the apple is soft but not breaking up. Add the basil. Remove from the heat and set aside until cold.
3 Carefully remove the apple segments from the syrup and place in a bowl. Pour the syrup through a sieve onto the apple. Serve chilled with cream or yoghurt.

NUTRITION PER SERVE
Protein 0.5 g; Fat 0 g; Carbohydrate 51 g; Dietary Fibre 3 g; Cholesterol 0 mg; 834 kJ (199 cal)

STORAGE: Store for up to 4 days in an airtight container in the fridge.

Cook the sugar and water until the mixture becomes a deep caramel color.

Arrange the orange slices, slightly overlapping, in the dish.

GRILLED ORANGES WITH CARAMEL MINT BUTTER

Preparation time: 20 minutes
Total cooking time: 20 minutes
Serves 4

6 oranges
$\frac{1}{3}$ cup (90 g/3 oz) sugar
3 tablespoons cream
45 g ($1\frac{1}{2}$ oz) unsalted butter, chopped
2 teaspoons grated orange rind
2 tablespoons finely chopped fresh mint

1 Peel the oranges in a circular motion, cutting only deeply enough to remove all the white membrane. Cut the oranges into thin slices.
2 Place the sugar and 3 tablespoons water in a small pan. Cook over very low heat without boiling until the sugar has dissolved (shake occasionally but do not stir). Increase the heat and bring the syrup to the boil. Cook until deep golden. Remove from the heat and gradually add the cream (the mixture will become lumpy). Return to the heat and stir until the caramel dissolves.
3 Add the butter, orange rind and mint to the pan and whisk until blended. Transfer to a bowl and chill.
4 Preheat the grill. Arrange the orange slices slightly overlapping in a 23 cm (9 inch) round shallow ovenproof dish. Dot with the caramel butter and grill until the butter has melted and the oranges are hot.

NUTRITION PER SERVE
Protein 2 g; Fat 16 g; Carbohydrate 36 g; Dietary Fibre 4 g; Cholesterol 49 mg; 1215 kJ (290 cal)

Fruit Ice Blocks

An ideal way to finish off a barbecue, especially if there are hungry children invited, is with a colorful array of fruit ice blocks. You can buy ice block moulds (like ice trays but with separate handles for freezing in the moulds) at supermarkets. All these fruit ice blocks will keep in the freezer for up to 3 weeks (although the mango and raspberry blocks are best eaten the day they are made), but they taste so good it is pretty certain they won't last that long.

PINEAPPLE AND MINT ICE BLOCKS

Purée 500 g (1 lb) fresh pineapple flesh and 10 fresh mint leaves in a blender or food processor until smooth. Sweeten to taste with 1–2 teaspoons caster sugar. Pour the pine- apple purée into 6 plastic ice block moulds. Freeze for 30 minutes, add the ice block sticks and return to the freezer. Freeze for a further 2½–3 hours, or until the ice blocks are frozen solid. Makes 6

PEACH AND YOGHURT ICE BLOCKS

Peel and remove the seeds from 6 ripe peaches and purée the flesh in a blender or food processor. Add 2 tablespoons plain yoghurt and mix well. Sweeten to taste with 1–2 teaspoons caster sugar. Pour the mixture into 6 plastic ice block moulds and freeze for 30 minutes. Add the ice block sticks and refreeze for 2½–3 hours, or until the ice blocks are frozen solid. Makes 6

GINGER AND LYCHEE ICE BLOCKS

Combine ⅓ cup (90 g/3 oz) sugar and 1 cup (250 ml/ 8 fl oz) water in a small saucepan. Bring to the boil and stir over medium heat until the sugar dissolves. Boil for 5 minutes, then remove from the heat and add 1 tablespoon chopped fresh ginger. Set aside for 10 minutes. Strain into a bowl, add 1 tablespoon lime juice, cover and chill until cold. Pour into 4 plastic ice block moulds and freeze for 1 hour. Add 6 seeded and chopped lychees, add the ice block sticks and freeze for 2½–3 hours, or until frozen solid. Makes 4

BERRY ICE BLOCKS

Purée 300 g (10 oz) mixed berries in a blender until smooth (reserving a few berries for decoration if you want). Push the mixture through a sieve and add 2 teaspoons lemon juice. Sweeten to taste with icing sugar. Pour the mixture into 4 or 6 plastic ice block moulds, dropping any reserved berries into the mixture, and freeze for 30 minutes. Add the ice block sticks and refreeze for 2½–3 hours, or until the mixture is frozen solid. Makes 4–6

MANGO AND RASPBERRY ICE BLOCKS

Peel 2 large mangoes and purée the flesh in a blender or food processor until smooth. Add ¼ cup (60 ml/2 fl oz) orange juice, mix well and pour into 4 or 6 plastic ice block moulds. Randomly add 4–6 raspberries into each mould as you fill them. Freeze for 30 minutes, add the ice block sticks and freeze for a further 2½–3 hours, or until frozen solid. Makes 4–6

WATERMELON AND KIWI FRUIT ICE BLOCKS

Purée 300 g (10 oz) seeded watermelon pieces in a food processor or blender until smooth. Sweeten to taste with 1–2 teaspoons caster sugar. Peel and slice 2 kiwi fruit and place the slices decoratively on the inside wall of 6 plastic ice block moulds. Pour the watermelon purée into the moulds and freeze for 30 minutes. Add the ice block sticks and freeze for a further 2½–3 hours, or until frozen solid. Makes 6

Ice blocks, from left: Pineapple and Mint; Peach and Yoghurt; Ginger and Lychee; Berry; Mango and Raspberry, Watermelon and Kiwi Fruit

USEFUL INFORMATION

The recipes in this book were developed using a tablespoon measure of 20 ml. In some other countries the tablespoon is 15 ml. For most recipes this difference will not be noticeable but, for recipes using baking powder, gelatine, bicarbonate of soda, small amounts of flour and cornflour, we suggest that, if you are using the smaller tablespoon, you add an extra teaspoon for each tablespoon.

The recipes in this book are written using convenient cup measurements. You can buy special measuring cups in the supermarket or use an ordinary household cup: first you need to check it holds 250 ml (8 fl oz) by filling it with water and measuring the water (pour it into a measuring jug or even an empty yoghurt carton). This cup can then be used for both liquid and dry cup measurements.

Liquid cup measures

1/4 cup	60 ml	2 fluid oz
1/3 cup	80 ml	2 1/2 fluid oz
1/2 cup	125 ml	4 fluid oz
3/4 cup	180 ml	6 fluid oz
1 cup	250 ml	8 fluid oz

Spoon measures

1/4 teaspoon	1.25 ml
1/2 teaspoon	2.5 ml
1 teaspoon	5 ml
1 tablespoon	20 ml

Nutritional information

The nutritional information given for each recipe does not include any garnishes or accompaniments, such as rice or pasta, unless they are included in specific quantities in the ingredients list. The nutritional values are approximations and can be affected by biological and seasonal variations in foods, the unknown composition of some manufactured foods and uncertainty in the dietary database. Nutrient data given are derived primarily from the NUTTAB95 database produced by the Australian New Zealand Food Authority.

Oven Temperatures

You may find cooking times vary depending on the oven you are using. For fan-forced ovens, as a general rule, set oven temperature to 20°C lower than indicated in the recipe.

Note: Those who might be at risk from the effects of salmonella food poisoning (the elderly, pregnant women, young children and those suffering from immune deficiency diseases) should consult their GP with any concerns about eating raw eggs.

Alternative names

bicarbonate of soda	—	baking soda
capsicum	—	red or green (bell) pepper
chickpeas	—	garbanzo beans
cornflour	—	cornstarch
fresh coriander	—	cilantro
cream	—	single cream
eggplant	—	aubergine
flat-leaf parsley	—	Italian parsley
hazelnut	—	filbert
jaffle	—	toasted sandwich
plain flour	—	all-purpose flour
prawns	—	shrimp
rocket	—	arugula
sambal oelek	—	chilli paste
snow pea	—	mange tout
spring onion	—	scallion
thick cream	—	double/heavy cream
tomato paste (US/Aus.)	—	tomato purée (UK)
kettle barbecue	—	Kettle grill/Covered barbecue
zucchini	—	courgette

Weight

10 g	1/4 oz	220 g	7 oz	425 g	14 oz
30 g	1 oz	250 g	8 oz	475 g	15 oz
60 g	2 oz	275 g	9 oz	500 g	1 lb
90 g	3 oz	300 g	10 oz	600 g	1 1/4 lb
125 g	4 oz	330 g	11 oz	650 g	1 lb 5 oz
150 g	5 oz	375 g	12 oz	750 g	1 1/2 lb
185 g	6 oz	400 g	13 oz	1 kg	2 lb

2006 Barnes & Noble Publishing

ISBN-13: 978-0-7607-8294-1
ISBN-10: 0-7607-8294-6

Printed and bound in China by Toppan Printing Co. Ltd.

10 9 8 7 6 5 4 3 2 1